THE HILL
Its History - Its Recipes

by Eleanore Berra Marfisi

Petti di Vitello Ripieno, page 141

G. BRADLEY PUBLISHING, INC. • ST. LOUIS, MISSOURI 63131

Publication Staff

Author: ....Eleanore Berra Marfisi
Copy Editors: ....Gloria Baraks
....Blake Baraks
....Faye Venegoni
....Meg Kane
Book Design: ....Diane Kramer
Color Photography: ....Voyles Studio/Jim Kersting
Photo Design: ....Michael Bruner
Dust Jacket Design: ....Michael Bruner
Project Coordinator: ....Brad Baraks
Publisher: ....G. Bradley Publishing, Inc.

Dedication

It is with overwhelming pride for my Italian ancestors that I dedicate this book to the early immigrants whose indomitable spirit led them to embark on a new life; leaving their home, friends, and family. After overcoming all the odds against them, they not only bettered their own lives–they have ultimately enriched ours and, indeed, the City of St. Louis.

Please check the G. Bradley Publishing Web site to review other Midwest history books such as this:
www.gbradleypublishing.com

Copyright 2003 by G. Bradley Publishing, Inc. All rights reserved. Printed in the United States of America. No part of this publication may be reproduced, stored in a retrieval system, or transmitted, in any form or by any means, electronic, mechanical, photocopying, or otherwise without the prior permission of the publisher.

ISBN 0-943963-96-6
Printed in the U.S.A.

Table of Contents

Introduction	4
Foreword by Mayor Francis Slay	5
Chapter One: A New Life	6
Family Recipes	26
Zuppa Inglese	28
Risotto Milanese	29
Eggplant Balls	30
Caponatina	31
Ravioli	32
Mec e Lach	33
Cannoli alla Siciliana	34
Polenta and Rustida	35
Cassata Cake	36
Italian Seed Cookies	37
Sicilian Village Dish	38
Torte di Riso	39
Roast Chicken with Lemon	40
Hot Penne with Mushrooms	41
Pasta con Fagioli	42
Basic White Sauce/Simple Sauce	43
Pasta Recipe	44
Crostoli	45
Sicilian Braciole Farsumagru	46
Chicken Cacciatore	47
Sicilian Spinach Pie	48
Casseoula (Cassera)	49
Arancini	50
Melanzane Involtini	51
Chapter Two: Times Moves On	52
Restaurant Recipes	116
Charlie Gitto's Recipes	118
"The Original" Toasted Ravioli	120
Veal Nunzio	122
Risotto with Fresh Tomatoes	124
Eggplant Parmigiano	125
Bone-In Fillet	126
Fresh Stuffed Tilapia	128
Chocolate Caramel Cheesecake	129
Charlie Gitto's Lobster Spedini	130
Tenderloin Stuffed with Lobster	132
Fresh Tomato and Zucchini Bruschetta	132
Veal Chop Milanese Style	133
Penne Borghese	133
Dominic's Recipes	134
Zuppa di Pesce	136
Ossobuco	138
Roast Lamb alla Romana	140
Petti di Vitello Ripieno	141
Fettuccine alla Bolognese	142
Zuppa per le Feste	144
Giardinello Grilled Eggplant	145
Tiramisu	146
Farfalle alla Karman	148
Petti di Pollo alla Gina	148
Spaghetti with Basil and Tomato Pesto alla Jackie	149
Spaghetti with Broccoli and Shrimp alla Maria	149
Giovanni's Recipes	150
Braciole di Pescespada	152
Veal Saltimbocca alla Giovanni's	154
Zucchini Ripiene di Carne	156
Vitello con Melanzane	157
Melanzana alla Conca D'Oro	158
Farfalline del Presidente Reagan	160
La Ribollita	161
Ossobuco Milanese	162
Risotto con la Zucca	164
Crema al Mascarpone	164
Calamaretti delle Marche	165
Spaghettini Aromatici	165
Cunetto's Recipes	166
Linguini Tutto Mare	168
Cavatelli con Pomodoro	170
Linguini alla Pavarotti	172
Lentil Soup	173
Bistecca alla Siciliana	174
Spaghettini con Broccoli	176
Chicken Spedini	177
Chicken Marsala	178
Ditalini con Piselli	180
Chicken Cardinale	180
Minestrone Soup	181
Chapter Three: The Now Years	183
Contributors	196
Acknowledgements	197
Epilogue	199

HISTORY | *The Hill*

INTRODUCTION

The production of the *The Hill: Its History, Its Recipes* was a mixture of dedicated work, fascinating interviews with Hill residents, visually stunning photographs, and our simple enjoyment of the subject material. From the outset, the book's identity was a concern for me. How much should we emphasize each aspect of the Hill with its traditions, its food, and its people? The book ended up similar to its subject–multifaceted. The Hill is a community steeped in Italian history. Without profiteering, there is a strong sense of wanting to keep their grandparent's traditions and memories close by. In the three history chapters, you can follow a timeline beginning with their immigration from Italy, then moving to their immersion into American society, their neighborhood's growth, and subsequent refinement.

Without boasting, the Hill is a location which possesses some of the finest Italian restaurants in the country. Four of the best are Charlie Gitto's "On the Hill," Dominic's, Giovanni's, and Cunetto House of Pasta who have all contributed some of their most popular recipes. As an added bonus, we asked 24 inhabitants of the Hill to share their favorite passed-down-from-Grandma family recipe. While working on this project, our entire production staff found it nearly impossible to control the urge to begin cooking Italian meals.

For clarity, the reader might note the following technique we used while designing this book. In the three history chapters, the words set in brown type were used to set apart quotations extracted from the author's extensive interviews of Hill residents. These quotes have not been credited to a particular individual since they are common "Hill stories," known by many from the area.

Surrounded by a major American city, the Hill neighborhood is unique since, unlike similar neighborhoods which have either dispersed or been consumed by the larger city around them, it possesses an internal strength. What is the glue which has held it together over the decades? In my opinion, there are several reasons: Most importantly, its neighbors care for each other unconditionally. Centered around the strength of the Church, its parishioners serve others faithfully. Without being elaborate or showy, people from the Hill embody a quiet confidence which lies at the heart of the community's self-reliance and independence. It was these factors, among others, which gave the book a unique voice; so that you, the reader, might feel as if you're hearing these stories from the perspective of an actual Hill resident. I hope you enjoy *The Hill* as much as we have.

Brad Baraks, Publisher

Foreword

The Hill is a tight-knit neighborhood with character; a people with a strong sense of community, rich in history and civic pride. It is where residents can walk to church or to their favorite grocery store, bakery, or restaurant. It is where children walk to school or to Berra Park for a game of baseball or soccer. The Hill is where everyone looks out for one another.

While it has recently become more ethnically diverse, it retains a strong sense of family. Manicured lawns, tree-lined streets, and brick bungalows are indicative of their sense of stability and a deep knowledge of their own special identity.

The past and present strengths of the Hill are, without a doubt, the seeds of St. Louis' revitalization: a pride of place, a love of family, and a focus on what is unique about city living.

This volume, *The Hill: Its History, Its Recipes,* takes us on a wonderful journey through the streets of the Hill and into the hearts and homes of its people.

Francis G. Slay
Mayor
City of St. Louis

HISTORY | *A New Life*

Left: The Restelli family stand outside of their home in Baggio, Milan, Italy. Baggio was one of the many rural towns in the Lombard region. Many of the Hill's residents emigrated from Lombardy.

Right: Pictured are Mr. and Mrs. Joseph Ceriotti and their children (L-R) Louis, Harry, and Anna. These early immigrants were willing to work hard to provide for their family and to ensure a promising future for their children.

The Hill area is seen below in 1875. With relatively few homes built, the brick and clay operations occupied most of the available property. Companies like Laclede Fire Brick Works, Pacific Fire Clay Works, Mitchell's Fire Brick Works, St. Louis Smelting, and Cheltenham Fire Brick Works are scattered throughout this early sketch.

Chapter One: A New Life

"They had a hard life in Italy. They also had a hard life on the Hill. But here there was opportunity; there was a future."

The Hill is truly a prime example of the American success story. Christopher Morley may have captured the essence of the Hill community when he wrote:

"To be deeply rooted in a place that has meaning is perhaps the greatest gift one can have. If that place has a feeling of permanence, it may well give to each citizen a sense of identity."

This feeling of belonging and this sense of identity did not come without a struggle. This history is a saga of what the hard-working, strong-willed Italian immigrant strived to achieve.

Life in Italy during the mid-1800s was difficult. Opportunities for advancement were neither available nor possible since Italy's economy was largely based on a feudal system. The nation's wealth was essentially controlled by landed proprietors who were considered to be aristocrats. In Northern Italy they were referred to as the aristocrati, and in Southern Italy they were called signori.

Families were forced to indenture their children for menial wages. These landlords would exploit the peasants by demanding they work long hours under extremely poor conditions. Sons labored in sulfur mines, breathing toxic fumes which sorely jeopardized their health. Daughters were sent to work in rice fields and silk factories.

"When my mother was only ten years old, she worked in a silk factory. She worked ten or twelve hours a day, start-

Having emigrated from Ossona, Italy, Mr. and Mrs. Giovanni Bismaro pose with their children for a family portrait.

Relatives in America were happy to receive a photograph sent from Sicily of Mr. and Mrs. Fudano with their daughter.

Angelina Colombo is photographed with her brothers (L-R), Battista and John. The picture was sent to their friends back in Marcallo, Italy.

HISTORY | A New Life

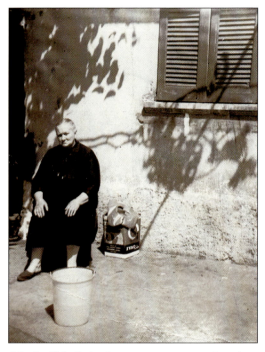

Maria Chiodini takes a moment to rest from her many chores in Marcallo, Italy.

ing at five in the morning. Her job was to reach into vats of boiling water to pull the silk from the silkworms. She often went to work without eating, but sometimes the padrone (overseer) would give her and the workers something to eat."

To ensure their survival, it was essential for families to have their children find employment. Since girls were expected to marry and raise a family, a formal education was deemed unnecessary, so it was never considered.

While growing up, sons painfully realized that there was only a small chance they could improve the status of their family. They could not hope to own land. Everything was controlled by the upper classes, the aristocrati. For young men, education was also out of the question since they were needed and expected to help support their family. The Italian government pressured young men to serve in the army to fight land wars in the African Campaign. In order to escape the rigors of the war, many would leave their Italian homeland for the shores of America.

"In my early childhood, I learned of the horrors of war from my father. He was in the Italian-African Campaign from 1895 to 1896. He was captured and held prisoner for over a year at which time a part of his right ear was bitten off. He told me this was done to the men to mark them as a prisoner. He later befriended a young African girl who helped him escape. He walked miles through the mountains until he reached the coast and

Young farm hands load the hay in Marcallo, Italy.

Washing clothes by the river was truly a difficult chore for young women in Italy.

Taken in 1950, Senora Teresa Piantanida rides her cart as she delivers "rags" in Ossona, Italy.

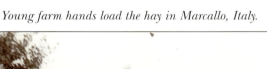

boarded a tramp steamer back to Italy. King Victor Emmanuel awarded him the Medal of Honor for his service to Italy and his king."

Harsh working conditions, demanding overseers, low pay, and few opportunities for advancement were reason enough for restless young Italians to wish and to dare to seek brighter horizons. After the unification of the Italian peninsula in 1861, over sixteen million Italians emigrated to other parts of the world. Cheaper tickets for steamship passage would also help in making the emigrants dream a reality.

"When my grandmother came to America in 1905, she was only twelve years old. She often told us about her trip from Genoa to America. It took her father a long time to save up enough money for her ticket. At the time, it cost only $28 in American money. She lamented that 'it was no fun and cost too much.' She slept on a narrow bunk bed which was crowded and not too clean. Besides getting seasick during thunderstorms, she was also very sad. 'I cried, I was scared ... too young, too far.'"

This photo shows the historic bridge in Casteletto, Cuggiono, Italy.

Bottom Left: Benedetta Sudano-Mocca proudly poses with members of the Mocca family in America.

In the 1860s, many northern Italians from Venice, Piedmont, and Lombardy emigrated to Argentina and Brazil. However, from 1886 to 1890 there was a sharp increase in Italian emigration to the United States. During this period, the greater number of those traveling to the United States were from the Island of Sicily.

Surprisingly, emigration was actually encouraged by the Italian government since their economy was in a deplorable state. With Italians leaving their homeland, it would ease the problem of overpopulation. Money earned abroad could be sent back to families and eventually back into Italy's economy.

The area in St. Louis to which many of them would come, now called the Hill, was at first remote and uninhabited. It was originally a part of the Charles Gratiot's League Square which the Spanish Territorial Government granted to Gratiot in 1798. However, by the middle of the nineteenth century, it was sub-

divided into large tracts and sold off by the Gratiot heirs.

Within the limits of the present Hill area, owners of the larger tracts were Peter Lindell, Henry Shaw, J.F. Cooper, and Mrs. Frances Sublette. At the time, much of this area was considered a wasteland. However, the discovery of valuable clay deposits in the 1830s was a major factor in the growth of the Hill community. These discoveries encouraged English Quakers to come to the area in 1844, opening the first clay products plant. Around this time, large veins of soft coal were also discovered. The clay and coal mines drew many immigrants from Germany along with African Americans who first inhabited the Hill. The mines were their opportunity to seek employment.

In 1853, Etienne Cabet, a French Utopian socialist, led a group of 200 followers called Icarians. Cabet was a man of many talents. He was a politician, writer, lawyer, and a propagandist. Cabet's group purchased 28 acres of ground on Wilson Avenue, east of Sulphur. It was here they built a communal center and several small cabins. Together, their community enjoyed such cultural pursuits as drama, music, and literature. However, Cabet's experimental settlement was a failure. It was abandoned in 1865 because of dissension, malaria, and financial difficulties.

In 1890, both the Frisco and the Missouri-Pacific Railroads began running through the northern portion of the Hill. Train travel through the area became a catalyst for business growth. Terra cotta, brick, and clay industries profited as they were established directly along the railroad tracks. Due to the expansion of these industries, there was an increasing need for labor which drew large numbers of Italian immigrants to the Hill. The geographic location of the Hill in the City of St. Louis is bounded by Kingshighway, Northrup, January, and Southwest Avenues.

In 1911, Ciro and Sam Tornetto take time out to relax in their backyard.

Below: Early 1900s St. Ambrose Sunday School teachers volunteered their time to teach the children of the early Hill immigrants.

From 1880 to 1895, records indicate the names of the first Italians who settled on the Hill were: Luigi Oldani; Domenico Taveggia; Luigi Caloia; Paolo Re; Luigi, Enrico, and Carlo Berra; Luigi Giacomo; Carlo Gualdoni; Abramo, Carlo, and Angelo Calcaterra; Cesare Oldani; Dionigi Puricelli; Domenica Miriani; Allesandro Chiodini; Calogero Mugavero; Pietro Mazzola; and Theodore Brusatore.

Having previously worked the mines in Italy, it was natural for the Italian immigrant to seek the work that was familiar to them. And so, after emigrating to the United States, they found employment in the Illinois coal mines.

"When my father left Casteltermini, Sicily in 1908, he was seventeen years old. Traveling with a group of friends, they were cleared on Ellis Island and took a train to Pennsylvania where they worked in a coal mine. When they heard that the working conditions in White Ash, Illinois were better, they left Pennsylvania. After that, they came to St. Louis because they heard it was easier working in the clay mines. But my father always said that it wasn't better since it was dirty and hard. He had a hard time breathing with all that dust in his lungs. Some guys even died from it."

Several major clay mines and brickyards offered employment to the Hill immigrants. Among them were: Laclede-Christy, on Chippewa; Laclede #1, at Wilson Avenue near Sulphur; Evans & Howard, located on Manchester; and Blackmer-Post on Columbia and Hereford.

While the mines provided essential work for the immigrant, they were usually a less than desirable place of employment. The men would load the clay in cars, receiving 40 cents for every car they filled. They worked under dangerous conditions, constructing wooden beams in order to keep shelves of limestone from caving in on them. If they had a good day, they could load nine or ten tons which amounted to $4 per day. Despite the fact that their work was demanding and pay was meager, they were required to supply their own picks and shovels.

"In 1910, my father worked twelve hours a day, six or seven days a week for $1.50 a day. His job was dangerous. After they drilled holes in the clay, my father would fill them with dynamite. After the dynamite exploded, he would

Top Right: (L-R) Saverio Monaco and his "compare" (friend), Nicola Carosello, stop to greet each other before their long and dangerous hours working in the mines.

Men from the Hill receive the Laclede-Christy Safety Award for working several years without an accident.

HISTORY | A New Life

help clear out the clay. When my father was injured, they made him stay home since he couldn't work. He had no insurance, so I had to quit school in the seventh grade and find a job."

A great number of these brave Italian pioneers were bachelors. They came to escape the poverty and hardship they were forced to endure in their native land. They desired to build a new life for themselves and their family. What better place to do this but in America – and on the Hill! So they journeyed here, filled with dreams of a better life.

Needing a place to stay, these young men became boarders with other families. Some homes could have as many as nine or ten boarders at one time. Money earned from these men also served as a means of support for the host family. They slept in cramped quarters, often on cots, with five or six to a room.

"My grandmother did not want my father to come to America because he was so young, only eighteen years old. But she finally gave him permission to go. When he arrived in the fall of 1907, he stayed with three other boarders on Pattison. They all slept in one room. Every fifteen days they pitched in to buy food at the Italian co-op at 5200 Shaw. His first job was at Green's, a division of Laclede-Christy located just north of the Hill, near the River Des Peres. My dad worked two or three days a week, ten hours a day for 15¢ an hour. He pushed a wheelbarrow carrying a load of 60 bricks. Later in 1910, he went to work for Evans & Howard Pipe Company, near the intersection of Macklind Avenue and Manchester Road. His job was to put clay pipes into hot ovens and remove them when they were baked. It was hot, dangerous work but at least his new job paid 25¢ an hour, and he worked six days a week!"

Dominic Miriani, grandfather of Bill Bartoni, poses for a formal picture postcard, taken circa 1895.

Eventually, the married men would send for their wives. Others went back to Italy to marry, later returning with their brides. Young bachelors would encourage their girlfriends to travel to St. Louis so they could get married here. It was not uncommon for parents to choose a bride for their sons, often someone their son had never met. The families would send photographs across the ocean so the future couple would recognize each other when they finally met! However, not every young Italian girl was so obedient and docile, especially when she was in love.

"My father had a young Italian boy picked out to marry my sister, Frances. But my sister was strong-willed and loved another young man of German extraction. In order to

In the early 1900s, the Tornetto family enjoys a backyard party. For many Hill families, the presence of family, friends, and music was all they needed for an enjoyable evening.

stop my sister from seeing her young love, my father moved our entire family to Joliet, Illinois. But my sister didn't stay in Joliet, going back to the Hill to marry the man she loved. My father learned a lesson: Do not attempt any more matchmaking with his other daughters. In fact, when he walked me up the aisle on my wedding day, he whispered to me, 'If you change your mind, it's okay; we'll have a nice party anyway.'"

By 1900, the Sicilians and southern Italians arriving on American shores outnumbered those from Lombardy and northern Italy, even though both would settle on the Hill. Language, customs, and historical differences caused a rift between the Lombards and the Sicilians. Therefore, it was not unusual for problems to arise when these two cultures clashed.

"They didn't get along. Lombards didn't want their sons to marry a Sicilian. Sicilians didn't want their daughters to marry a Lombard. We even had different clubs to socialize in. The Lombards had the Big Club Hall, which was a grocery co-op only for the northern Italians. The Sicilians had the Palma Augusta, where they held their meetings, weddings, and various social events."

While differences did exist, it would only be a matter of time before the old hostilities would eventually dissipate.

In the early twentieth century, the Hill was geographically isolated from mainstream St. Louis life, lying close to the city's western border. City services such as paved streets, sewers, and streetlights were non-existent.

"My grandparents settled on the Hill in 1901. My nonna (grandmother) used to tell us stories about life back then. When it rained, it was difficult to walk in the mud, so they stretched boards across the dirt roads. She had to hold on to wooden fences along the way just to keep from slipping into deep holes in the mud."

In 1905, Father Cesare Spigardi, a gentle and unassuming priest, entered the lives of the Hill's Italian residents. He empathized with the troubles they were experiencing as they were trying to find a place for themselves in the fabric of American life. He understood the need to bring unity and strength to this small community. And so, in 1907, Father Spigardi sent to Italy for Father Carotti to minister to the Hill community. The Church would be the glue that would ultimately bind this community together.

Father Carotti's work encompassed many facets of their lives. He initiated a cooking class for young women. He made arrangements for adults to attend English classes. Embroidery classes were held for anyone who wished to attend. The Church became the nucleus of the immigrants' lives. The interest and enthusiasm of Father Carotti encouraged the Hill's ancestors to tack-

Mary Valloni-Torno's Immigration Identification Card, dated 1929. Mrs. Torno was only five years old when she arrived in New York.

Reverend Julius Giovanni (third from left) and Charles Gioia (third from right) gather for a photograph in 1910.

HISTORY | A New Life

le each problem with undaunted determination and fervor.

They built homes, paved sidewalks and streets, and brought plumbing into their homes. Their work ethic was the impetus which made the Hill a viable part of the City of St. Louis. Daily, these tired and weary men would trudge up the steep, muddy hill on their way home from the mines. Since they believed the Hill was the highest point in the City of St. Louis, they referred to it as La Montagna (The Mountain). One can easily understand their struggle, perhaps even have compassion for them. After ten or twelve hours of hard labor, their trek home certainly must have been similar to climbing an actual mountain!

The women did not find life any easier than the men. Their lives were also harsh and difficult.

"Life was hard. Everything which needed to be washed, had to be done by hand on a board. You couldn't put them outside to dry, because they would freeze and be stiff as a board. Instead, we used to hang a clothesline in the kitchen, keeping our clothes there until morning when they'd be dry. For light, we had only a lantern with coal oil in it. It was a rough life. Thank God we had a coal stove, a bucket of coal, and a boxful of wood to start a fire in the morning, otherwise we would all freeze. As far back as 1915, my mother would cook over a coal stove everyday. Our meals were simple. The only meat we ever ate was rabbit since we were too poor to buy our own meat. My brothers would go rabbit hunting, my father would skin them, and my mother would cook them in a stew.

We were crammed into three rooms without a basement, hot water, or plumbing. My mother never wasted anything. If bread was left over, she made it into bread crumbs. I remember my father breaking hard bread into a bowl of coffee for breakfast. My father used to bring home cement sacks from work. After scraping the cement off, my mother would wash and scrub them until they were clean. Then she made underslips, aprons, and dish towels out of them. She wasted absolutely nothing."

Small businesses began to appear between the years of 1900 and 1920. It was during this period when the Hill became literally self-sufficient. These mercantile establishments were started out of necessity to meet people's basic needs. Shoe repair shops, bakeries, grocery stores, taverns, movie theatres, barbershops, drugstores, a funeral parlor, dry goods and furniture stores, and even their own brass band were introduced on the Hill.

"In the years before there was a funeral parlor, when somebody died, they kept him in their house. That was terrible,

Salvatore Russo cannot hide his love for his little daughter, Tina.

Mrs. Giovanna Lange proudly poses with her son, Louis.

though, since you couldn't go in that room for a week. Every time one of us kids went inside that room, we felt like the dead body was still there. We sure were glad when Paul Calcaterra opened up the first funeral parlor."

Italian immigrants had to overcome difficult conditions, working hard to make a better life for their families.

"In 1917, during World War I, water pipes had to be laid in Illinois from Belleville to Scott Field. My father was one of the Italian work crews recruited by the United States government for the job. He and his crew worked so well that they were sent to Fort Knox in Louisville, Kentucky to lay pipes. Their next stop was close to Youngstown, Ohio to put in water pipes for a small arms plant there. Our government must have certainly recognized that he was dependable and unafraid of hard work, even if it meant being away from his wife and children."

In spite of these hardships, people still found time for simple enjoyment.

"We were poor, but we still had good times. We had wedding parties in the backyards, with people playing mandolins and accordions. Sometimes we celebrated for three or four days. Every household had little lanterns burning in the backyard, and on weekends we would all get together. The men would be out there playing cards, singing, and drinking beer. We used to sing a lot."

The Hill was truly a self-sufficient small town in a large city. In spite of being surrounded by clay mines, factories, railroad tracks, and the River Des Peres, the Hill quickly became independent. The Hill community gave the Italian immigrant "a feeling of permanence and to each a sense of identity."

Top: (L-R) Josephine Cucchi, Angelina Gioia, and Emilia Garavaglia don their favorite hats for a studio photo.

Left: Hill backyards served as playgrounds for neighborhood children.

Right: (L-R) Serena Fontana, Caroline Merlo-Gianino, and Josie Oldani-Merlo enjoy a sunny afternoon with their children.

History | *A New Life*

Celebrating their class reunion in America are Albino Pozza and Louis Pisani (front row, center).

The Church on the Hill

In 1903, the Hill community witnessed the birth of Saint Ambrose Church. It all began when a gentle priest, Father Cesare Spigardi, entered the lives of the Hill's Italian immigrants. He believed he was given a divine challenge to found a church for them. A small, white frame structure with a single, tall steeple marked the birth of Saint Ambrose Church. In 1905, Father Spigardi appointed Father Lucian Carotti to be the first pastor of Saint Ambrose Church.

However, the people of Saint Ambrose suffered a serious loss on January 20, 1921 when their tiny, frame church was destroyed by a fire. A temporary chapel was set up at the Salus Infirmorum Church on Shaw Avenue. Fortunately, Saint Ambrose's congregation had purchased the property from the members of the old German Protestant Church in 1919. These strong-willed immigrants would not allow their hope of having their own church to be shattered. They stressed the need to unite, to be determined, and to erect a new church–not built with wood, but of bricks! They encouraged one another to look upon this venture as a noble cause, perhaps even the will of God.

Father Carotti emphasized that this was to be a collective effort, involving every family in the parish. Angelo Carrubia was chosen as the architect and Casagrande & Spezia were the contractors. On September 12, 1921, the

A century ago, this small, white frame church was built in 1903, with a single, tall steeple marking the birth of St. Ambrose Parish.

HISTORY | *A New Life*

In the early 1900s, (L-R) Reverend Cesare Spigardi and Reverend Giulio Giovannini pose with St. Ambrose parishioners, Catechetical instructors, and lay personnel of St. Ambrose School.

Below: In 1906, Reverend Lucian Carotti sits among St. Ambrose's children on the day of their First Communion in front of St. Ambrose School, located on Cooper (Marconi) Street.

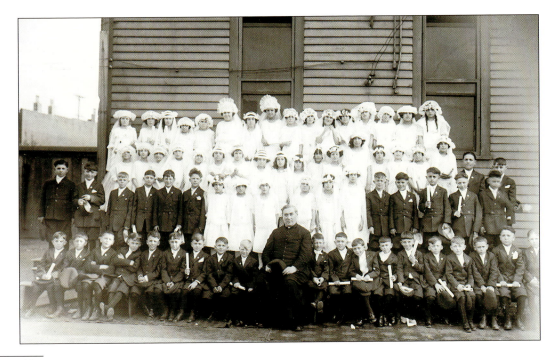

excavation of the church's basement was begun. Along with the Hill's immigrants, Father Carotti's tireless efforts to make this dream a reality involved hardships, privations, and long hours of work for everyone. This would ultimately play havoc with Father Carotti's already frail health. In an attempt to regain his strength, he returned to Italy much to the sadness of the parish.

Giulio Giovannini was then appointed administrator of Saint Ambrose Church. His genuine sincerity succeeded in uniting the parish. He constantly urged them to focus on their ultimate goal; to complete the work they had begun. Children saved up their pennies so they could buy a brick for ten cents. Men donated many hours of labor. Anyone who contributed to this great endeavor would have a star placed on the church's ceiling. Each star would be a testament to their faith in their priest, their community, and their God. Since no church could be complete without a bell, Father Giovannini suggested that the bells be imprinted with the Italian cities which the immigrants came from. The parishioners were so moved by this idea that enough money was raised to order five bells almost immediately. Each bronze bell held the following inscriptions:

The people of the Parish. . .
to Saint Ambrose
The faithful of Cuggiono. . .
to Our Lady of Mount Carmel
The faithful of Inveruno. . .
to Saint Theresa
The faithful of Marcallo. . .

A New Life | HISTORY

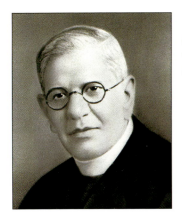
Reverend Cesare Spigardi

Reverend Lucian Carotti

Reverend Julius Giovanni

St. Ambrose Church's steel structure stands majestically in the center of the Hill.

HISTORY | *A New Life*

to Saint Nazario
The faithful of Casteltermini. . .
to Saint Vincent Ferreri

The five new bells rang out joyously for the first time on Sunday, June 13, 1926. Modeled after the Basilica of Saint Ambrose in Milan, the structure was designed in the magnificent style of Lombardy Romanesque. At 10:00 A.M. on June 27, 1927, His Excellency Archbishop John J. Glennon presided over dedication ceremonies for Saint Ambrose Church. Gala festivities were held throughout the parish. People danced, sang, and hugged for it was the birth of the glorious parish which would embrace the entire community. Each heart swelled with loving pride for the fervor of their founding fathers, for the ingenuity and foresight of Angelo Corrubia who designed Saint Ambrose, and, above all, for their faith in each other and in God.

Saint Ambrose Church was the glue which held the community together. It not only gave the Italian immigrants spiritual strength and a place to worship, it became the focal point for countless celebrations. Joyful festivals were held on various feast days, held in honor of Saint Sebastian, Saint Rosalia, Our Lady of Mount Carmel, Saint Joseph, Saint Dominic, and Corpus Christi. Each feast had its own festival replete with various booths and crafts. These celebrations would continue throughout the evening with eating, drinking, music, and games. Today, parishioners of Saint Ambrose continue this tradition by celebrating the feast of Corpus Christi, which honors Christ, and the feast of Saint Joseph, the protector of our families.

On June 13, 1926, St. Ambrose Church was completed and its five bells rang out for the very first time.

A New Life | HISTORY

The interior of St. Ambrose Church was designed similar to the magnificent churches in Lombardy. Its architectural style is Romanesque, modeled after the Basilica of St. Ambrose in Milan.

In 1926, St. Ambrose's First Communion Class has its picture taken shortly before the blessing and installation of the church's five bells.

HISTORY | A New Life

The Sisters of Loretto, who staffed St. Ambrose School, pose in 1919 with students and parish priests for the annual school picture.

PATTISON AVENUE NEGRO BAPTIST CHURCH

Barely known by most St. Louisans, the Pattison Avenue Negro Baptist Church once existed on the Hill. They met in a tiny, light gray frame building on the 5200 block of Pattison, nestled between a group of homes occupied by African-American families who had settled on the Hill prior to the arrival of the Italian immigrants. Each Sunday, the church would bring together worshippers from all sections of the City of St. Louis for services.

The congregation was organized in 1897. It remained in existence until 1970, when its building site became part of the right-of-way for Interstate 44.

OTHER CHURCHES

The Italian Evangelical Church, taken in 1929.

ITALIAN EVANGELICAL CHURCH

The Italian Evangelical Church was founded in 1908 by Reverend Peter Ottolini, an Italian Protestant minister. Reverend Ottolini held services in various residences on the Hill, converting a few families to Protestantism. The congregation's first church was built in 1917 and was located at 2109 Edwards Street. In 1929, the Italian Evangelical Church moved to 5343 Botanical Avenue. In recent years, it found another home on Tesson Ferry Road and is now known as the Evangelical Full Gospel Assembly. Currently, the church building houses the Basuk Baptist Church. Its members are predominantly Korean-Americans with services held in the language of their homeland.

Reading and Writing

Saint Ambrose School

In January 1906, fifty boys and girls registered at Saint Ambrose School. The school building consisted of two rooms and only children in the primary grades were accepted. The older children attended Shaw School. After the school had been open for two years, the enrollment increased considerably so another classroom had to be added. Up to this time, few of the Hill's children advanced beyond the fourth grade. They went to work at an early age because they were needed to help support their families. Another disadvantage was their lack of exposure to the English language.

As the population of the parish grew, the need for a larger school became apparent. Once again, the energy, will, and creative power of the Hill's inhabitants rose to meet the challenge. In 1915, a new school and convent were built under the direction of Father Luciano Carotti. The sisters from the Order of Saint Theresa staffed the school from 1916 to 1919. The Sisters of Loretto succeeded them in 1919, remaining on staff until 1941. In 1941, the Missionary Zelatrices of the Sacred Heart (now known as the Apostles of the Sacred Heart of Jesus) served as staff for Saint Ambrose School.

In the early 1940s, the need for a still larger school became sorely apparent. However, the financial setbacks of the Depression and the outbreak of World War II prevented school administrators from making their dream a reality. With determination, their perseverance and stamina would once again come to the surface and, in April 1950, the current school building was dedicated.

Henry Shaw School

The Henry Shaw School was opened in 1870, beginning in a two-story frame building at Kingshighway and Vandeventer Avenue. It held only four rooms and had a seating capacity of 240 pupils. It was relocated to its current site on Columbia Avenue in September of 1907. During that school year, enrollment swelled to 928 students, which included 85 children born in their Italian homeland. By 1914, this number grew to 258. However, the number of students who were the children of immigrants was approximately 900. In 1915, evening classes for adults were introduced at the Shaw School and 153 Italian immigrants registered to study English as a second language.

Theresa Carnaghi, second grader, sits attentively in the front row (at right) in the old St. Ambrose School.

HISTORY | A New Life

Relative to today's standards, the tuition at Saint Ambrose School was miniscule, but still many families could not afford to send their children there. As a public institution, the Henry Shaw School was able to give children in these families a first-class education.

For African-American students, a public school was established on the Hill in 1901. Located at 5326 Northrup, it was named after two educators, John and George B. Vashon, who fought to ensure civil and human rights for African Americans across the nation. In 1910 the school was discontinued, but the name was later revived by the City of St. Louis when Vashon High School opened on September 6, 1927.

In 1915, the new St. Ambrose School was completed on Wilson and Hereford Streets.

Below: The Henry Shaw Elementary School. "Mr. Kerr, our principal, held a very structured program at Shaw. We didn't have time for extra-curricular activities because we had to hurry home to do our chores."

The Volstead Act and the Hill

When the Volstead Act was made into law, the Prohibition Era began and St. Louis was considered to be the epicenter of the illegal liquor trade. The press, however, did a great disservice to the Hill community regarding its involvement in unlawful activities. Newspaper articles had given erroneous and unjust impressions about the Hill's Italian immigrant families engaging in the "bootlegging" industry. This form of notoriety stigmatized the Hill as a "rough and dangerous neighborhood."

"I attended Rosati-Kain High School, and my friends could never come over to my house because I lived on the Hill. Their parents wouldn't allow them to visit because they believed it was too dangerous. They wouldn't even let them walk across Kingshighway!"

Admittedly, a few families did engage in producing illegal alcohol on the Hill. They even developed complex systems in their homes, using their sub-basements to connect with tunnels running under the roadway. This was also a convenient method for transporting sugar, a necessary ingredient for distilling alcohol.

"When I was a kid, I thought it was really exciting to see moonshine flowing down the streets and into the gutter when the firemen pumped liquor out of basements and into the sewers. Then, they would connect the hoses to the fire truck and pump water down into the sewers. It didn't scare us, we just thought it was really interesting."

Another memory: "As a young girl, my girlfriend and I were playing in her basement on a Saturday afternoon. I was about nine years old, and I was intrigued with the huge pool in the center of her basement. When I went home, I asked my mother why we didn't have a swimming pool in our basement. She made me promise never to go near that 'pool' again because it was too dangerous. It wasn't until I was older when I realized it was a huge vat where my friend's father used to make moonshine."

In those days: "My uncle was out of work and he needed help to support his family. So when he was approached by a neighborhood acquaintance to have sugar stored in his home, my uncle agreed. He was happy to let him do it since he was going to pay my uncle for 'renting' his basement. But one evening, he and some friends were enjoying themselves by singing and playing the piano, when all of a sudden someone knocked on the door. When my uncle opened the door, some guy handed him a note and walked away. There was nothing written on the note, only a symbol with two black hands. My uncle knew right away the danger he was in. A symbol made with two black hands (Mani Neri) meant that, if he continued to store the sugar, the 'Mani Neri' would harm him or his family. For Italian immigrants, black hands meant dirty hands. It wasn't long before my uncle stopped storing sugar."

Old times: "Those moonshine days were awful, particularly for families who only wanted a small amount of alcohol. My neighbor made moonshine in his basement. He was a nice man and he would give us a dime if we helped carry the sugar into his garage. My father didn't make whiskey, but he did make wine just for us. Most of our friends made wine too, but they didn't sell it. All of my friends grew up with wine on the supper table. When my father poured us a glass of wine, he would always water it down with a lot of white soda."

What one must understand is that, while a few families did make moonshine, the negative public stereotype of the Hill as a hotbed for bootleggers stemmed mainly from violent criminals from downtown Chicago and St. Louis. These were the people who would frighten and coerce hard-working immigrants and small business owners into paying for protection.

The Hill's Italian immigrants, as illogical as this may seem to mainstream thinking in modern America, did not look upon their involvement as illegal. To them, it was simply an additional means of livelihood for their families.

FAMILY RECIPES

Similar to the restaurants they live by, many Hill families find time to cook succulent Italian meals for their loved ones. Hill residents take pride in their heritage, and there are few things more Italian than a fine dining experience. What follows are 24 family recipes which have been handed down for decades. As you prepare these marvelous dishes, many of these skilled household chefs want to encourage you to experiment with their recipe, so as to "make it your own." They further explain, "The basic elements for creating flawless Italian meals is taste and technique. This is the method used by our families. It's the way my mother taught me, the same way her Mom taught her. Our kitchen shelves weren't crammed with cookbooks, recipe cards smeared with fingerprints, or ragged pages torn from culinary magazines. We just cooked."

RECIPES | Family

ZUPPA INGLESE

Zuppa Inglese (literally "English Soup") is the Italian equivalent of trifle, a dessert created in the British Isles. I first enjoyed it at my cousin Maria's house in Italy about forty years ago, then adapted it for use here. It not only looks elegant but tastes delicious and is simple to prepare.

INGREDIENTS

1 box chocolate pudding
1 box vanilla pudding
1 pkg. frozen strawberries, thawed
1 pkg. ladyfingers, about 20
rum or amaretto
1/2 pt. whipping cream

Prepare pudding as directed. Dribble rum or Amaretto over ladyfingers. In plain glass bowl, arrange ladyfingers on the bottom and sides. Place 1/2 of strawberries over the ladyfingers on the bottom. Ladle in vanilla pudding. Place rest of strawberries on top of that. Ladle in chocolate pudding. Whip cream adding 1/2 teaspoon vanilla and two tablespoons powdered sugar. Spread over chocolate pudding. Nuts may be sprinkled on top. Refrigerate. Serves 8 to 10.

GLORIA GRIFFERO

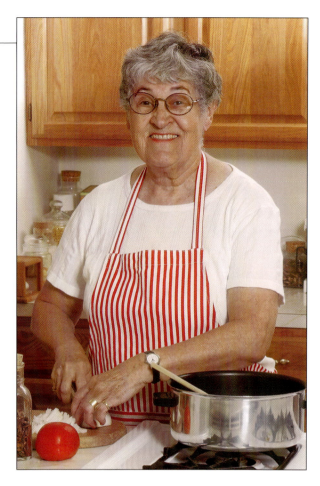

"As in every Italian family, Mom did all the cooking, although Dad did teach her how to make ravioli and Genovese pesto for her gnocchi. He also made 'stociofisso' (dried cod) which he soaked for several days under running water, then cooked with anchovies and oil.

Mom's dishes were simple and hearty. Unfortunately, I wasn't interested in cooking then but I did learn how to make risotto as she did—I still have the wooden spoon that she used—and homemade pasta.

She wasn't a baker. She only made 'turtui' (apple fritters) on Fridays, which we dipped in sugar or dropped in our coffee.

We shopped at Gioia's Grocery Store where we had a running account that we paid monthly. The garden tended by my Dad provided vegetables, as did street vendors. Bread was delivered daily by Rebon, a neighborhood baker.

Mom bought live chickens and killed them by wringing their necks. We ate practically all of them, feet and gizzards included. Occasionally, we raised rabbits, which found their way to our dining table.

The table always included wine made by my father every year in the basement."

Family | RECIPES

RISOTTO MILANESE

INGREDIENTS

1/2 stick butter (1/8 of a pound) salted
1 medium yellow sweet onion
1/2 lb. gizzards (cleaned and sliced in small bits)
1 package porcini mushrooms
4 oz. dry white wine
2 cups of long grain or Italian short grain "arborio" or "carnaroli" rice
4 to 5 cups chicken stock
1 cap or 1 envelope Zafferano (saffron)
1/2 cup grated parmigiano cheese
salt to taste

In a four-quart pot: sauté the chopped onion in butter (1/2 stick) and cook till translucent (do not brown). Add gizzards and cook, add mushrooms and stir in with sautéed onion and gizzards. Mushrooms are first soaked in water to reconstitute and wash. They are strained of water and cut finely and added to onion and cooked together for flavors to blend–for about three or four minutes on low heat.

Add rice mixture and stir together and toast for two to three minutes on low heat.

Add wine and stir together for flavors to blend. Turn up heat to medium-high and add hot chicken broth (enough to cover rice) and stir continually till broth is absorbed then add more broth. (Add in saffron to cooking rice at time of adding broth in order for saffron to dissolve.) Add salt to taste as needed.

Cooking time is about 20 minutes. When cooking, rice broth is always added gradually till absorbed and then additional is added. Rice should have enough heat to cause small bubbles to appear in mixture. Heat must be regulated as needed. Note when stirring the cooking rice be sure not to let rice stick to the bottom of the pot. When cooked, the rice grain should be slightly chewy. Stir in half of the grated cheese before serving and let cooked rice rest in pot for two or three minutes (no heat) before placing rice on serving platter. Also sprinkle cheese over plated rice.

ROBERT RUGGERI

WHY IS RISOTTO MILANESE A "GOLDEN" COLOR?

While there may be debate in some circles as to whether zafferano (saffron) is only a coloring or if it adds a taste to food, there remains an undisputed fact as to the reason saffron is used in the Risotto Milanese recipe. During the Renaissance period the very wealthy Milanese used fine layers of gold leaf to top their dishes. The poor Milanese started using saffron to mimic the gold effect of gold topping.

RECIPES | Family

EGGPLANT BALLS

My uncle planted a garden every spring. And in the summer he would supply us with wonderful vegetables. My brother and I loved eggplants. They were our favorites. So my mother would always make eggplant balls! They do not take much time to make and they are delicious!

INGREDIENTS

2 eggplants
2 eggs
chopped parsley
minced onion
1/2 cup grated cheese
bread crumbs
salt and pepper

Peel two eggplants. Cut into cubes and cook in boiling water until tender. Drain. When cool press out excessive water. In a bowl add: eggplant, two eggs, a little chopped parsley, a tablespoon of minced onion, 1/2 cup grated cheese, salt and pepper to taste, and enough bread crumbs to hold the eggplant mixture firm.

Form into balls and fry or bake in a greased pan at 350 degrees for about 18 minutes. Serve with or without sauce as an appetizer or side dish or serve with spaghetti in place of meat balls! Eggplant gives a great flavor to the sauce.

MARY CALCATERRA

Family | RECIPES

CAPONATINA
(Eggplant Appetizer)

Ingredients
1 large eggplant
1/2 cup plus 2 tbsp. olive oil or salad oil
2 1/2 cups sliced onion
1 cup diced celery
2 (8 oz.) cans tomato sauce
1/4 cup red wine vinegar
2 tbsp. sugar
2 tbsp. drained capers
1/2 tsp. salt
12 pitted black olives in slivers

I learned this recipe from my mother, Serafina Giordano. She came from Casteltermini, Sicily in 1890. It was the custom of her town to serve Caponatina on St. Joseph's Day. So when she came to America and started a family she continued the tradition. I was the middle child of nine children. I started cooking when I was ten to help my mother.

Wash eggplant, cut into 1/2-inch cubes. In 1/2 cup hot oil in large skillet, sauté eggplant until tender and golden brown. Remove eggplant and set aside. In two tablespoons hot oil in the same skillet, sauté onion and celery until tender–about five minutes. Return eggplant to skillet, stir in tomato sauce, bring to boiling. Lower heat and simmer, covered, 15 minutes. Add vinegar, sugar, capers, salt, pepper, and olives. Simmer covered and stirring occasionally for 20 minutes longer. Refrigerate covered overnight. Serve with toast rounds or crackers.

Mary Zagarri

"My sisters and I, and our friends on the block, would play Bat and Ball, only we used a broomstick because we didn't have a bat. We had a lot of fun.

On Sundays, my mom would send us to the movies, which were three blocks from my house. It was called the Columbia Show. She would give us fifteen cents; ten cents for the show and five cents to spend. I would buy a box of cheese bits.

We had Angelo's Restaurant down the corner and Ruggeri's up the block. Ruggeri's started a birthday club, so on our birthdays Mom would send my sisters and me there.

Mom used to shop at George Oldani's grocery store. He would bill her every day and then at the end of the month she would pay him. Missouri Bakery was very good to Mom, too. She would buy a fifty-pound sack of flour and make her own bread and noodles."

RAVIOLI

Meat Filling
2 lbs. roast beef
2 lbs. chicken breast
4 carrots
3 stalks of celery
2 onions
2 tbsp. salt and pepper
1/2 cup olive oil
1 large bag frozen spinach thawed
4 eggs
1 1/2 cups Italian bread crumbs
1/4 cup romano cheese

Dough
3 1/2 cups semolina flour
5 eggs
1 1/4 tsp. salt
3 tbsp. oil
water

Homemade Meat Sauce
1 lb. ground beef
1 small can of tomato paste
32 oz. tomato sauce
1 stick of butter
1/4 cup oil
2 carrots, finely chopped
1 onion, chopped
1/2 cup parsley
2 cloves garlic
3 cans of mushrooms or 1 lb. fresh sliced mushrooms
salt and pepper to taste
1/2 cup romano cheese
1/2 cup water

For the past 60 years, Sunday dinners with Grandma and Grandpa were always special. They were traditional! Our entire family—children, grandchildren, and great-grandchildren sat around the huge round table every Sunday. It was where Grandpa told stories and Grandma smiled! We shared more than good food and great stories. We learned about our ancestors and were encouraged to try their recipes. Ravioli was one of our favorites. My son and I continue to keep this tradition alive because in doing so we also keep our family close which was really Grandpa's plan more than a half century ago!

To prepare meat filling cut beef and chicken into small cubes and place in a large pot. Pour warm water over the meat until the meat is covered. Sauté onions, celery and carrots in two tablespoons of olive oil. Add to pot with meat. Season with salt and pepper to taste. Boil meat and vegetables for 2 1/2 hours. Let cool. Finely grind meat and vegetables. In large bowl, put meat mixture, spinach, eggs, bread crumbs, romano cheese, and a half cup of olive oil. Mix the ingredients well by hand.

Combine ravioli dough ingredients—flour, eggs, oil, and salt—and mix by hand in large mixing bowl. Add small amount of water if dough is too dry. If the dough is too sticky, add more flour. On a floured surface, knead the dough well. Form into a large ball. Cover the ball with a wet towel and let the dough stand for 40 minutes. Uncover dough and roll out as thin as possible. Begin spreading meat filling on 1/2 of the dough with a large spoon. Try to spread ingredients evenly and approximately 1/8 inch thick. Then gently lift the other half of the dough and place it over the filled side. Mark off your dough into two-inch squares. Using a pastry wheel, cut along the two-inch lines. Place cut ravioli on a floured piece of waxed paper. The ravioli may be cooked at this time or frozen for cooking at a later date.

TO COOK THE RAVIOLI: Bring three quarts of water to a boil. Drop ravioli carefully into the boiling water and cook for approximately eight minutes. Cooking too long will cause your ravioli to fall apart. Drain the ravioli and add your favorite sauce, or homemade meat sauce. Sprinkle with grated parmesan cheese.

MEAT SAUCE: In large pot, cook ground beef, onion and garlic in oil. When beef is browned, add all other ingredients and simmer together for four hours.

LANCE BERRA AND SON, LAWRENCE

Family | RECIPES

> "My parents, three brothers and I were lucky to have a farm, so even in the worst of times we had food for the family and to share. During World War II there were many German soldiers quartered in our town in Italy and my mother had to cook for many of them. While we knew she hated doing this, they never suspected. She could have won an Academy Award for her acting!
>
> From watching my mother I always knew the importance of using herbs in cooking and I still grow many of my own. The addition of herbs can really help a "poor" meal.
>
> We made our own salami, copa and prosciutto. We also made our own wine. One of my favorite memories is of being sent to the basement to get wine for each meal. But, my father wanted me to whistle the whole time so he knew I wasn't down there drinking!"

INGREDIENTS

4 qts. Italian buns or bread torn into small pieces
8 oz. amaretti cookies, crushed
2 qts. whole milk
4 eggs
1/2 lb. raisins (I use more)
1 tbsp. vanilla
1/2 cup sugar
  (approximate – use to taste)
1/2 cup unsweetened cocoa
1/2 cup pine nuts, toasted
grated rind of one lemon
1/2-1 stick butter, sliced into pats

MEC E LACH (BUNS AND MILK)

This Italian chocolate bread pudding recipe was traditionally made in September for the feast of St. George, the patron Saint of Bernate Ticino (a small town near Milan, Italy).

Combine all ingredients except butter. Note: I don't pour all the sugar in until I have tasted to see if it needs the entire half cup. Mixture should be more liquid than solid. If bread has absorbed all of the milk, add a little more. Coat deep, wide casserole pan with butter or spray with Pam. Pour into prepared pan, dot top of casserole with butter pats working a few down into the mixture. Bake at 350 degrees for approximately one hour and then check (a deep pan may require a little more oven time). Cool completely and store well covered in refrigerator. Keeps for weeks. Note: This has turned out just a little differently every time we make it. Sometimes the cookies are more or less sweet so you might need more or less of the sugar. I like a lighter chocolate and my wife, Julie, a darker so we compromise on the cocoa. Just taste it and adjust before you place in the oven.

ERMANNO IMO

RECIPES | Family

CANNOLI ALLA SICILIANA

This is a double treat from Sicily: crisp fried pastry and creamy ricotta. Either one could definitely stand on its own, but combined they become cannoli. The pastry was once fried wrapped around pieces of canna (bamboo cane), hence the name "cannoli." Today we substitute (for the cane) one-inch aluminum piping available at Italian markets on the hill. The Sicilian style had distinct Arabian origins. This spiced pastry roll stuffed with ricotta was originally quite different. The Arabian style was a banana stuffed with almonds, sugar, and dried fruits. "Some people put diced candied fruit in the cannoli stuffing, but I prefer just the chocolate," notes Dora.

CANNOLI SHELLS

1 egg, well beaten
1 tbsp. melted butter
Enough vegetable oil for deep-frying
3 tbsp. sugar
1-1/2 cups sifted flour

CANNOLI FILLING

12 oz. ricotta cheese
2 oz. bittersweet chocolate chips
1/2 cup confectioners sugar
cinnamon, a dash

Shells: Combine eggs and melted butter. Add sugar and beat well. Add flour. Mix until it holds together in a ball. Roll out on floured board to paper thinness. Cut into 6 x 4 inch ovals. Bring two long sides together and fasten at the center by moistening edges with water. Fry in deep fat until golden brown.

Filling: Put ricotta through sieve. Combine ricotta with sifted sugar. Hand mix well with vanilla, chocolate chips, and cinnamon. Refrigerate until ready to use. Use pastry bag to stuff shells.

Fills six shells.

DORA DIGREGORIO

> Sam DiGregorio became frustrated one Christmas when he saw that all of his family were eating in different rooms–some in the kitchen, some in the dining room, some in the living room. He set about to make a huge table in the basement of the house that was able to seat all of the family. Through the years, this table held a special significance for the DiGregorio kids.

POLENTA AND RUSTIDA (CORNMEAL AND MEAT STEW)

This is a hearty main dish from Lombard region, usually served in winter. The rustida may be prepared ahead of time and reheated but the polenta should be made just before the meal.

RUSTIDA

1 3/4 lbs. extra lean pork tenderloin
3/4 lb. luganiga (Italian sausage found in Italian markets)
1 lb. garlic salamini (Italian sausage found in Italian markets)
3 1/2 lbs. onions, thinly sliced
1/2 to 3/4 cup red wine
1 can (28 oz.) tomato sauce
3 tbsp. tomato paste
3 or 4 cloves, whole
Optional: salt and pepper to taste (Note: the sausages are seasoned)

POLENTA

3 cups polenta (cornmeal)
8 cups water or chicken broth
1/2 stick butter
1/2 cup grated parmigiano cheese
salt to taste

Cut all the meat into one inch pieces. Sauté in a small amount of butter until all of the meat is browned. Add the sliced onions, wine, tomato sauce, and the tomato paste. Also add in the gloves at this time. Bring to a boil, then turn down the heat. Simmer for one and a half hours. After letting it cool, store in the refrigerator overnight then remove the excess fat.

Polenta: Blend water and corn meal, then bring to a slow boil. Stir constantly for about 25 minutes. Add the butter and cheese. Stir for another five minutes until the butter and cheese are completely dissolved into the polenta. Cover to keep warm, then serve with the rustida. Polenta is extremely versatile, as it becomes complementary to the flavor of the dish it accompanies. With a swirl of gorgonzola cheese, polenta can be simple meal on its own.

Optional: Serve the above with a green salad in a vinaigrette dressing and a bottle of red wine. Top it all off with macedonia (a fresh fruit salad) sprinkled with sugar and a little red wine or sweet liqueur.

Serves 8 to 10.

JULIA PASTORI

RECIPES | Family

Cassata Cake

I learned this recipe from my mother-in-law, Pauline Privetera Giuffrida, who emigrated to the United States from Augusto, Sicily in 1920. This is a wonderful dessert to be used on any occasion.

Ingredients

1 small pound cake sliced thin, 1/4 inch (you can use a pound cake you bake or buy fresh or frozen)
1/2 gallon whole milk
2 cups sugar
1 1/2 cups cornstarch
1/4 tsp. cinnamon oil (purchase at Italian import stores)
1 orange rind washed, peeled from orange in one piece if possible
1 tsp. vanilla
shaved chocolate from a candy bar (cold)
red maraschino cherries cut into 4 pieces each

Slice the pound cake first and line the bottom of a 9 x 13-inch pan with half the pound cake slices. In a pot big enough for all the remaining ingredients, pour the milk into the pot reserving two cups. Add the sugar, cinnamon oil, the orange rind and vanilla. Turn the heat on and stir contents. Mix the cornstarch into the remaining two cups of milk. Stir until there are no lumps. Let the milk warm. After the milk gets warm remove rind and add the stirred milk and cornstarch stirring constantly. Do not stop stirring or lumps will occur. When the mixture boils cook one more minute. Remove from the heat immediately and spoon half the mixture over the pound cake, then take the rest of the pound cake and layer it on the hot mixture. Then spoon remaining pudding on top of the pound cake. Spread evenly. Immediately press cherries in a spaced design on top and then sprinkle on shaved chocolate. Refrigerate immediately. Serves 15.

Jean Giuffrida

Italian Seed Cookies

This cookie recipe is being shared in loving memory of my mother, Katie Brusatori. It is only one of many things she taught me as a child growing up on the Hill. These cookies were made and enjoyed in our home on Sundays, at holidays, and especially during the Christmas season. Hopefully, these cookies will be enjoyed for generations to come, and a little bit of my mother's spirit will also be shared with you and your family.

Ingredients

1 lb. sesame seeds
2 cups flour
1/2 cup Crisco
1/2 cup sugar
2 tsp. baking powder
2 eggs
1 tsp. vanilla

To prepare, beat eggs then add Crisco, sugar and vanilla. Combine baking powder and flour. Add flour and baking powder, a little at a time to the eggs, Crisco, sugar, and vanilla mixture, mix well. Roll out like a breadstick. Prepare a dish with a little milk, and a dish with seeds. Cut roll into three-inch long sections; dip into milk and then into seeds. Put on greased cookie sheet. Cook until brown, approximately 25 minutes at 350 degrees.

Donna Kemper

SICILIAN VILLAGE DISH

Cooking has always been an important facet of our family. Cooking for thirteen—two parents and eleven siblings—made cooking more interesting and a challenge, especially during the Depression era. Yet we all survived. My dad was a much better cook than my mom. However, my sister, Phyllis, learned from both of them and became a cook extraordinaire. She seldom used a recipe, except for baking. Her cookies and cakes and cannoli were exceptional. She told me that one needed a good imagination when cooking. She would tell me, put all the ingredients in your mind and if you think it will taste good, do it. She was right. Almost all that I learned about cooking I learned from my sister. I presently try other recipes and if I like the result, I continue to use them. I've cooked at St. Roch Catholic Church for the priests for more than 20 years.

INGREDIENTS
3 large white potatoes
2 large sweet potatoes
3 lb. salsiccia (Italian sausage)
1 large onion
1 med. can diced tomatoes

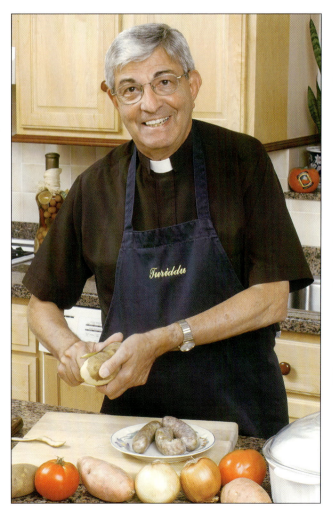

This is a hearty dish which is relatively simple to prepare. Also, by adjusting the amount of ingredients, it can serve a family or a small gathering. One-pot recipes, such as this one, are always favored by those given the clean-up duty.

Cut both types of potatoes into 3/4 inch squares and place them at the bottom of a roasting pan. As a second layer, arrange the sausage links on top of the potatoes. Cut the onions into thin slices and place them on top of the sausage links. Pour the can of diced tomatoes on top. Bake for one hour at 350 degrees. As it cooks, the juices from each ingredient drip down to season the potatoes. A wonderful taste.

Good for any season, this dish works best in winter, especially served with warm bread on a cold night. Serves 4 to 6.

MONSIGNOR SAL POLIZZI

TORTE DI RISO (RICE PIE)

In various villages in the Tuscany region of Italy, families gather to make this torte di riso or rice pie during the Easter season. I never saw a torte di riso in a bakery. They were always homemade. However, in Collodi, Italy, there is a festival in honor of Santa Maria which features these tortes. This is the only time of the year a person could actually purchase one. When my family and I emigrated to the United States from Lucca, Italy, we continued the Easter tradition of making the tortes. I will usually have them made by Good Friday but, of course, we cannot enjoy them until Easter Sunday. My children enjoy eating these tortes which they call "rice cakes" and look forward to them. They tell me it just would not be Easter without them. My children are now learning to make torte di riso so that they can continue the tradition for future generations.

FILLING
2 cups rice
4 cups water
4 cups milk
1/2 tsp. salt
1 1/2 cups sugar
6 large eggs
6 tsp. butter
1 tsp. vanilla
2 tsp. grated lemon rind
2 tbsp. sweet vermouth
2 tbsp. brandy

CRUST
3 large eggs
1 cup sugar
2 tsp. baking powder
1 tsp. grated lemon rind
3 1/4 cups flour
7 tbsp. butter, softened
1/2 tsp. salt

Filling: Cook rice with water, milk, and salt as instructed on the rice package. Let rice cool slightly and then add remaining ingredients. Let the filling cool, preferably overnight.

Crust: Combine all ingredients and mix to make a smooth ball. Divide ball into thirds. Roll each piece out to fit a nine-inch pie plate. Place crust into pie plate and fill with cooled rice filling. Make a decorative edge. (If you have excess crust you can make a lattice top for your pie or cut out a bunny using a cookie cutter to put in the center of your torte di riso.)

Place pies in a preheated 325-degree oven for 45 minutes or until crust is slightly brown. Makes three pies.

LAURA DELLA CROCE

RECIPES | *Family*

ROAST CHICKEN WITH LEMON

When our children come over for dinner, this is their favorite!

INGREDIENTS
1- roasting chicken 4 1/2 lbs.
2 large lemons thinly sliced
2 tsp. dry rosemary
1 1/2 tsp. salt
1/4 tsp. black pepper

Preheat oven to 450 degrees. Remove chicken gizzards and rinse chicken. Pat dry and place the chicken in a roasting pan breast side up. Gently loosen the skin from the meat, begin at the body cavity and work toward neck. Free the skin as much as possible without tearing. Rub the chicken meat underneath the skin with rosemary. Place lemon slices over the rosemary. Pat the skin back in place. Most importantly, sprinkle the skin with salt and pepper. Immediately turn down the oven to 350 degrees and roast for 20 minutes per pound. Serve with juices from the pan.

BEN GAMBARO

"Since I was born and raised in a family that operated a bakery, you would know I enjoy food. Spending 50 or 60 years in our shop, the Missouri Baking Company, helped my cooking. I became aware of how certain spices react in bakery mixes, so that when I cooked this knowledge helped. I don't recall my mother ever being considered a gourmet cook, but she certainly was a good cook. She cooked basic northern Italian food and believe it or not, we cooked at the bakery. I remember my uncle cooking large pots of risotto or baking a big fish in our oven. We would all sit down at the work bench and enjoy the food; family and employees alike."

Hot Penne with Mushrooms

This dish is a tradition in the Italian province of Lucca where an abundance of chestnut trees grow along the hillsides. Porcini mushrooms are found in the shady ground around these trees.

Ingredients
1/2 a red onion
5 tbsp. olive oil
2 oz. dried porcini mushrooms
1 tsp. red pepper flakes
4 tbsp. tomato paste
1 bouillon cube
1 lb. of penne pasta
parmesan reggiano cheese

To prepare, soak the porcini mushrooms in warm water. Finely chop the red onion. Put the olive oil in a pan, warming on stove top over low heat. Squeeze the excess water from the mushrooms, finely chop, sift together with the red pepper flakes. Place the onions in the pan and let them simmer for a few minutes. When they are crispy, but not brown, add the mushrooms. Simmer for a few more minutes while you stir together the mushrooms and onions. Add the tomato paste, which should be diluted with 1 1/2 cups of warm water. Add the bouillon and stir everything together. Cover saucepan, lower heat, and let simmer for about ten minutes or until all the liquid has evaporated. Continue to stir often.

Cook the pasta al dente (tender but firm) with salt water. After draining the water place in a bowl or put on the serving platter and add the sauce together with the pasta. Sprinkle parmesan reggiano cheese on top.

Assunta Della Croce

RECIPES | *Family*

PASTA CON FAGIOLI
(SPAGHETTI WITH BUTTER BEANS)

When we were little kids we had a lot of meatless meals. My mother was a good cook and she could make simple meals taste great. She never measured, she just knew how much to use. My brother and my sister and I convinced my mother to make the pasta with butter beans while we measured everything because it was one of our favorites. My mother learned from her mother in Palermo, Sicily, but we knew my mother added her own touch! I make this dish for my family and they enjoy it as much as we did!

INGREDIENTS

1/2 onion, diced

1/2 cup tomato sauce (puree)

1 cup butter beans cooked until tender or 1 can dry cooked butter beans (15 oz. can)

1/2 tsp. sugar

3/4 lb. spaghetti

1 tbsp. olive oil

Brown diced onions. Add 1/2 cup tomato sauce. Add butter beans and simmer about 15 minutes. Season with 1/2 teaspoon sugar. Add salt and pepper to taste. Cook spaghetti and drain. Add butter bean mixture and one tablespoon of olive oil. Stir and serve. Serves 4 to 6.

JOHN ITALIANO

Basic White Sauce / Simple Sauce

You can make a lot of different dinners using the basic white sauce recipe as a start. It's easy and delicious.

Basic White Sauce
1 stick melted butter
2 rounded tbsp. cornstarch
1/2 cup half-and-half

6-in-One Sauce (Simple Sauce)
3 tbsp. olive oil
1/2 large onion
2 cloves garlic
28 oz. can 6-in-1 brand tomatoes
1 tsp. sugar
5 fresh basil leaves

Basic White Sauce: Melt butter over low heat. Add two rounded tablespoons of corn starch and stir with fork. Add the half-and-half and stir over medium heat until it is nice and smooth (like soft pudding). That's all you need for basic white sauce. Now choose your favorite pasta dish.

6-in-1 Sauce: Put approximately three tablespoons of olive oil in skillet. Add 1/2 of a large onion and two cloves of garlic, sliced in 1/2 with the cut side in the oil. Soften over low to medium heat. Pour in one (28-ounce) can of 6-in-1 tomatoes. Rinse the can with about one inch of water and add. Add one teaspoon of sugar and about five fresh basil leaves. Simmer over medium heat for five minutes and it's ready!

This sauce is excellent over boiled ravioli. It can be made while you wait for the ravioli to cook. It tastes better than most commercial sauces, and it's soooo simple. You can also add pre-cooked salsiccia and peppers for a meat sauce over spaghetti. While fresh tomatoes may be used, 6-in-1 brand has a flavor that is extra good.

Diane Urzi

RECIPES | *Family*

PASTA RECIPE

The one thing in my life that has always made me feel truly Italian has been my family. Growing up, holidays were filled with the entire family gathering for celebrations, which usually revolved around food, and preparing the food was always much more than just a chore. Preparations involved several generations of women in my family coming together in the kitchen to artfully create meals to serve to dozens of people. As one generation would teach the next how to prepare recipes from our family's history, stories would be shared with one another about our origins. Now that key members of our family have passed on, and I have moved away from the remaining members, cooking is the one thing that always keeps me connected to my Italian family and heritage. I cook from recipes that are written in my grandmother's handwriting, as she looks over me from her photograph in my kitchen. This ritual helps to close the gap in the 2,000 miles between my ancestors and myself.

Now on weekends, I take the time to make pasta from scratch, as my grandmothers would have done. Taking care to mix the dough entirely with my own two hands to make sure that each piece of linguini or fettuccini is perfect.

INGREDIENTS
2-1/2 cups all purpose flour
1/2 cup of semolina flour
4 large eggs
1 tsp. salt

To prepare, mix together the dry ingredients on the kitchen counter and make a well with your fist. Crack the eggs into the well. Using your hands, carefully incorporate more and more flour to make the dough. Be warned! The dough mixture will become very messy and stick to your hands before too long, but remain patient and continue working with it until you have a ball of dough that is still soft but not too dry. You will most likely not use all the flour that the recipe calls for.

Let the ball of dough rest for 30 minutes under a bowl or damp towel, and reserve the remaining flour for dusting the dough as you go.

The next step varies depending on what you make but I use a hand-crank pasta machine to flatten the dough and then cut the dough into the desired pasta shapes.

Dry the pasta any way you please, but a laundry drying rack works very well! Mangia and enjoy!

ANNA ROSE VENEGONI

Family | RECIPES

Crostoli

There were no Christmas presents when I was a child. Mama managed to save extra money for the ingredients and the gallon of oil to deep fry the crostoli she made for us. Christmas was a joyous time. There was the family togetherness, visiting friends and relatives, and, of course, the huge platter of crostoli, a northern Italian treat. They were made during the winter, a time all homes could use the extra heat the frying would produce.

Ingredients
1/2 cup milk
1 stick butter
1 cup sugar
1 tsp. salt
3 eggs, stirred with a fork
1/2 cup whiskey
3 tsp. baking soda
flour

To prepare on low heat, melt butter and sugar in cool milk (not hot). Add rest of ingredients. Add enough flour till dough gets like pie dough. Knead dough till smooth. Roll as thin as paper. Cut in strips with fluted pie dough cutter. Tie in a knot or cut in diamond shape. Make a small cut in middle of diamond. Fry in hot oil as quickly as possible on both sides till golden brown. The longer in oil, the heavier and greasier the crostoli. Sprinkle with powdered sugar.

Note: Poor Mama worked to roll dough out the size of a tabletop to get it thin enough. Today with a pasta machine one can roll the dough with small pieces at a time. The machine rolls it thin and evenly.

Anna Lahrman

"It was the Great Depression and the Italian immigrants on the Hill, along with many others, were in desperate need. Barely speaking a word or two of English and with only his strong back and arms, Papa, like many others, couldn't find work. With a wife and four young children, Papa knew he had to provide food for us. He built rabbit hutches and raised rabbits in an old shed behind the house we rented on the 5200 block of Elizabeth Avenue. Mama had an art of cooking rabbit in many ways. We would eat polenta with stewed rabbit; with pasta or baked herbs and potatoes. Any way Mama prepared rabbit, the meal was fit for a king.

When I was 13 years old (I am now 72) my Papa gave me the job of caring for the rabbits. What my parents didn't count on was that I became very attached to them, making each one of them a pet and giving them all names. When Papa was preparing and skinning a rabbit for our next meal, I would run to the garage to see which one of my pets was missing. When supper time came, I refused to eat. I would only eat the pasta or bread.

RECIPES | Family

SICILIAN BRACIOLE FARSUMAGRU
(Falso Magro or False Lean)

My mother made this dish for special Sunday dinners. We were always excited when she did! My mother made sure she would have enough if anyone stopped over, and they usually did! Mama knew no strangers. She invited anyone who came to our door to sit at the kitchen table and share whatever she had prepared.

Ingredients
1 sliced round steak
1 cup seasoned Italian bread crumbs
1/2 lb. sliced salami
3 hardboiled eggs, cut in half lengthwise
parmigiano or romano cheese chopped
1 cup finely chopped onions or scallions
1 cup whole tomatoes squeezed over topping
salt, pepper, and granulated garlic to taste

To prepare, lay the round steak flat and sprinkle with salt, pepper and granulated garlic. Sprinkle seasoned bread crumbs on next and then layer salami on the steak. Place the hard-boiled egg yolk down on the steak and add the chopped onions. If using scallions, lay them across the steak alternating the green and white parts of the scallions. Spread the squeezed tomatoes over the steak. Leave about an inch along the edges of the steak when layering on the ingredients. Roll steak tightly and tie with a string. Brown the steak in a frying pan using olive oil. After browning, add the beef roll to your favorite pasta sauce with or without meatballs. Let the steak simmer in the sauce. Remove the beef roll from the sauce, leaving the string on, cut the roll into slices. Serve on a platter. Pour a little of the sauce over the top. Enjoy!

ANNIE GITTO

Family | RECIPES

Chicken Cacciatore

As a young girl, I learned from my mother as she was a great cook. My father also cooked, but mostly outside on the grill. He wasn't too shabby a chef, either. In my early years, we would shop at Mr. Italiano's market on the corner of Marconi and Bischoff. He always seemed to have everything a family like ours could ever need. When I was older, I was a cook at St. Ambrose School for fourteen years. I also had the opportunity to prepare meals for the priests at the St. Ambrose Rectory for twelve years.

Ingredients

8 pieces chicken
1/2 med. onion, chopped
4 cloves garlic, chopped
4 tbsp. oil
1 tbsp. parsley
1 tsp. oregano
1 tbsp. basil
1 can 15-oz. tomatoes, chopped
2 stalks celery, cut up
1/2 cup capers
12 olives – cut up in four pieces each
1 tsp. of salt
1/2 tsp. black pepper (or to taste)

Sauté onion and garlic in oil on not too hot of a fire. Put chicken in and stir it around for fifteen minutes. Put tomatoes in and stir it for about another fifteen minutes. Then add in celery, parsley, oregano, basil, salt, pepper, olives, and capers. Continue stirring. Now if it starts to get dry add in some water, don't make it soupy, just enough so it stays movable in the pot. Don't let it stick. Your best way is to let it simmer. It should be done in about 1 1/2 hours. Don't forget to stir it around.

Some nice fresh, warm, crusty Italian bread goes great with chicken cacciatore!

JENNIE RHODUS

RECIPES | Family

SICILIAN SPINACH PIE

This recipe was served by my mother on holidays and special occasions. It was actually one of my Papa's favorites. The spinach pie can be served as a great side dish or even a main meal, especially during the Lenten season. When served with a delicious garden salad, a side dish of olives and crispy garlic bread, complemented by a glass of red vino, this dish is pretty hard to beat!

INGREDIENTS

- 1 cup chopped onion
- 2 tbsp. olive oil
- 1 1/4 cup bread crumbs
- 1/2 cup grated romano cheese
- 1 cup tomato basil sauce (or 1 cup of your favorite red sauce – no meat)
- 3 – 10 oz. boxes frozen, chopped spinach
- 1 1/2 cups ricotta cheese
- 6 eggs
- 1 tsp. salt
- 1/2 tsp. black pepper
- 1 or 2 pinches red pepper flakes (optional)

Sauté one cup onion in two tablespoons olive oil until transparent. In a large bowl combine all ingredients plus the sautéed onions – mix well by hand. Spray ten-inch pie pan with Pam. Place mixture in pan and shape into pie shape. Bake at 350 degrees for one hour and 15 minutes (should be firm to touch). Cut into wedges and serve with extra red sauce and top with grated cheese. Mangia bené!

ADRIANA FAZIO

CASSEOULA (CASSERA) A STEW OF PORK RIBS AND SAUSAGES

This recipe of the cucina povera (kitchen of the poor people) was included on behalf of my dearly departed mother, Giuditta (Josephine) Pisoni, a great cook of Lombardian dishes.

INGREDIENTS
one pig's foot
2 tbsp. oil
2 oz. butter
1 diced onion
3 stems celery, diced
2 carrots, diced
1 pound luganiga or pork sausage
1 slab pork ribs, cut in half lengthwise (2 slabs baby back ribs may be substituted)
1 lb. pork skin
1 head Savoy cabbage cut into eighths
salt and pepper to taste

Boil the pig's foot and cut in two, lengthwise. Make a soffritto (sauté) with oil and butter and chopped onion until transparent. Add the pork meats, cut into pieces and add the pig's foot. When meat is golden brown, add the diced carrots, celery, and tomatoes. Cook over medium heat.

After 30 minutes, add the cabbage strips. Salt and pepper to taste and cook 45 minutes. The cooking liquid should be rather dense. (If you wish to remove some of the fat, do so before adding the cabbage.) Some water may be added during the cooking process if necessary.

Variation: Casseoula is a Lombardian dish that has many versions. Sometimes after the meats have browned, a spoonful of tomato paste is added. Other cooks prefer to cook the cabbage in a separate pot, steaming it in the water remaining on the leaves after washing, and then adding it to the meat. The quality of the meat added to the casseoula varies. The simplest version requires only ribs and sausage, while the most complicated includes the ears and tail. Polenta is the traditional accompaniment to casseoula.

DR. ROBERT PISONI

RECIPES | Family

ARANCINI (LITTLE ORANGES)

"The first time I tasted arancini, I was on a ferryboat traveling from the mainland to Sicily. I had never seen nor eaten them before this trip. I knew risotto was not used in the traditional Sicilian kitchen. So, it surprised me to see these rice croquettes, so golden brown they looked like little oranges. They were great! I now make them for every special holiday. While they are not the simplest to make, they are most delicious to eat!"

INGREDIENTS

1 cup Italian rice
saffron
1 cup seasoned bread crumbs
5 large eggs
1/4 lb. lean ground beef
1 small onion (diced)
5 large fresh sweet basil leaves (chopped)
2 tbsp. tomato paste
4 oz. tomato sauce
1/4 cup frozen or fresh peas
4 cloves of garlic
1/3 cup dry white wine
2-1/2 cups of water for rice
1/2 cup water for sauce
1 tsp. sugar
2 tbsp. butter
1 cup grated parmesan cheese
2 tbsp. extra virgin olive oil
2 cups vegetable oil
salt and pepper to taste

Melt butter in a large pot, pour in uncooked rice and cook for two minutes. Add in the saffron making sure it dissolves thoroughly. Pour in wine until wine evaporates. Begin stirring in boiling water until rice is tender. Cook rice uncovered. Add salt and pepper to taste. When rice is cooked take off heat, mix in cheese and two eggs. Place in refrigerator for two hours or overnight. Rice must be chilled.

In a large frying pan over medium heat add oil, sauté onions and the chopped garlic for two minutes. Add in the beef and pork, and brown. Remove excess grease. Add in basil, tomato paste, tomato sauce, water, and sugar until it all becomes thick in texture. Add peas while still warm, take off heat, and set aside. Add salt and pepper to taste.

Take two tablespoons of the rice mixture, place in hand and form a small cup. Place 1/2 teaspoon of the meat mixture in center of the rice cup, add one teaspoon of the rice over the meat mixture and roll into a ball. Roll the rice ball in the remaining eggs and then roll that in the bread crumbs. Heat vegetable oil to 360 degrees. Deep fry rice balls until browned, place on plate or dish covered with paper towels.

Before serving, garnish with cheese and/or the extra sauce.

REVEREND VINCENT BOMMARITO

Melanzane Involtini

My favorite memories are of my grandparents' home, with their garden and grape trellis in the backyard. Since we lived across the street, visits were frequent. The sidewalk was narrow and made of bricks, no doubt from the brickyard where my nonno, Vincenzo LoRusso, used to work. Summertime represented the best of times as bounties of stored recipes emerged. Nonno grew eggplants, Swiss chard, giant squash, tomatoes, peppers, and many herbs. Since my nanna, Sarafina LoRusso, passed away before I was born, some of the dishes I have learned were from my mother and aunts. Whenever nanna cooked, she was always thinking ahead. While preparing this dish, it offered her the time to make other items; meatballs, caponatina, and a tomato sauce. This time savings gave her a leg up on the first course of pasta, which she served only to nonno before every meal.

Sarafina almost always served this dish with pasta and the flavor combination is one that you will not soon forget. I prefer to serve this melanzane with fresh spinach. Buon appetito!

Ingredients
- 2 large eggplants – slice 1/4 inch lengthwise

Sauce
- 2 Italian whole peeled tomatoes (28 oz. cans) hand crush
- 2 tbsp. tomato paste
- 1 tsp. fresh basil
- 1/4 tsp. dry minced garlic (may substitute 1 tsp. fresh garlic)
- 1/2 tsp. pepper
- 1 tsp. salt
- 1/4 cup minced onion
- **You can increase your batch, and freeze for future use if desired.

Stuffing
- 2 lbs. ground chuck (may blend salsiccia with beef)
- 1/3 minced onion
- 1/3 cup parmesan cheese
- 1/3 cup Italian-seasoned bread crumbs
- 1/2 tsp. black pepper
- 1 tsp. dry minced garlic (may substitute 1 tbsp. fresh garlic)
- 2 tbsp. fresh minced parsley

Submerge sliced eggplant in salted cold water (one tablespoon per quart) for 20 minutes. Drain, rinse and pat dry. This can be done two days in advance. Spray slices with cooking spray and sauté two minutes per side to soften. Arrange on platter to cool. Combine ingredients to make sauce.

Stuffing: form a small egg shape with the meat mixture in your hand. Place a dime-sized piece of soft cheese (fontina or provolone) in the meat and close the mixture around it. Place the meat on one piece of cooled eggplant and roll. Place the roll seam side down in a 9 x 13 inch casserole dish that has been prepared with a layer of the sauce in it. Repeat placing eggplant rolls closely together until the dish is full. Gently, cover with remaining tomato sauce. Place strips of fresh yellow peppers on top of the eggplant.

Bake in oven for 45 minutes at 350 degrees. Allow dish to rest 15 minutes and serve with grated parmesan cheese.

Rich and Terri LoRusso

HISTORY | *Time Moves On*

Families on the Hill were often large in size. They lived in small homes and children often shared bedrooms, if not the beds. The kitchen served as the dining room, family room, and living room, all in one. While this may seem uncomfortable, it created a close family experience.

Below: Looking east on Pattison Avenue at Cooper (Marconi) Street in 1930 are rows of "shotgun houses" which had to be jacked up in order for the men to dig basements. Many were built from the wood used for the St. Louis World's Fair in 1904.

Chapter Two: Time Moves On

Life on the Hill in the 1930s was a period in need of recovery. As a result of the Great Depression, many of the men were out of work. Pride prohibited them from requesting relief from the government. However poor they were, the people on the Hill never really felt the sting of poverty. Their humble, three-room homes were called "shotgun" houses. It has been said that one could shoot a shotgun shell through the front door, and it would travel straight through the house and out the kitchen door. While their homes were small and often overcrowded, they were, for the most part, happy, close-knit families. During these transition years on the Hill, young people were the largest age group. In the 1930 census, the Hill's population had grown to 6,089, with almost twenty-eight percent between the ages of 5 and 20. "We never realized we were poor, because we were rich in so many ways. Life was safe on the Hill; we would sleep on the porch on hot summer nights. We walked to the Zoo or the Muny in Forest Park. We didn't need money. We would go to the Muny really early so we could see shows in the free seats. We had live entertainment on the Hill. I remember going to a carnival in Pattison Avenue's empty lot to watch the Zacchari Brothers get shot out of a cannon. We even had street dances. Although we lacked some material things, we gained in the sheer enjoyment of just being with friends. How lucky can you be? Only on the Hill!"

During World War II, the Hill responded to the nation's call to action, losing many of its fine young men in battle. To many, the 1950s was a "golden era," when life was lived as it should be.

The Italian immigrants, with the help of their friends, enlarged the otherwise small homes; adding basements, bathrooms, and a summer kitchen in the basement. Basement kitchens were popular since families could take refuge during the sweltering summer heat and humidity in St. Louis.

HISTORY | Time Moves On

FROM THIS DAY FORWARD

Italian traditions run deep. Time may have modified them, but their roots are strong. This is especially true for wedding customs, which are still continued today.

Courtships were considered to be a family affair. When a young man courted a young woman, it was understood that her older sister or a relative would accompany them on dates. Curfews were sacred. If her father said she had to be "in" by ten o'clock, it was not negotiable.

Before wedding arrangements were to be even considered, the boy had to first ask, and hopefully receive, permission from the girl's father. Fathers were very protective of their daughters, making sure that she would be well provided for if a union was to take place. Seeking permission continues to be a custom today, but it is seen more as a gesture of respect.

Mothers would begin to prepare for their daughter's wedding when the girls were only ten or eleven years old. Hours would be spent tediously sewing intricate cut-out work on embroidered pillowcases, napkins, tablecloths, and delicate designs for adorning nightgowns. These were some of the many items which would fill a young girl's "hope chest" (which the Lombards refer to as their daughter's "dote," meaning dowry). Mothers, aunts, and family friends would stitch, tat, and crochet to complete the future bride's trousseau. Special items made of silk and satin were often import-

Top Left: Theresa Maroni and her brother, Louis Maroni (couple behind chair), were wedding attendants.

Left: Mr. and Mrs. Vincenzo DiRaimondo are pictured with their friends during an elaborate wedding celebration.

Right: Mr. and Mrs. Luigi Berra (couple on right) are attendants for the wedding of Mr. and Mrs. Carlo Zarinelli.

ed from relatives who had remained in their Italian homeland.

Invitations to relatives were often hand delivered by the bride and groom. They would also give each relative a lovely present, which included candied almonds for tossing at the couple on their wedding day as a sign of fertility. The day before the wedding, the prospective couple and their bridal party met for a church rehearsal. Later, all were invited to a private dinner. After the wedding ceremony, the wedding party would leave St. Ambrose Church in a car decorated with white ribbons and bells. Their first stop would be to a local photographer for a formal studio picture. The next morning, after the wedding breakfast, everyone would ride together to visit relatives.

The wedding reception was always a gala affair. Paid for by the bride's parents, the traditional meal consisted of ravioli, roast beef, wedding chicken (baked chicken sprinkled with special spices), salad, and wedding cake for dessert. In addition, Sicilian brides would offer delicious cookies to each guest, baked by the mother of the bride from family recipes. Any food which remained from the reception feast was used for the "second day." This celebration would take place in a parent's home or backyard. With local musicians playing accordions, guitars, and mandolins, the second evening would be filled with lively singing and dancing.

The Charles and Annie Gitto wedding in 1953.

HISTORY *Time Moves On*

Mr. And Mrs. Joseph Tafuri

Mr. and Mrs. Anthony Merlo

Mr. and Mrs. John Anthony

Mr. and Mrs. Michael Columbini

Mr. and Mrs. Louis Brusatti

Mr. and Mrs. Angelo Berra

Time Moves On | HISTORY

Mr. and Mrs. Charles Grassi
Mr. and Mrs. Harry Brusatori

Mr. and Mrs. Vincenzo LoRusso
Mr. and Mrs. Carlo Bossi

Mr. and Mrs. Joseph Puricelli
Mr. and Mrs. Charles Garavaglia

HISTORY | *Time Moves On*

Mr. Carnaghi escorts his daughter Julia as her relatives break a dish, a traditional Italian "good luck" wish for the bride and groom.

Mr. and Mrs. John Zienta (bride and groom) greet friends and relatives in front of St. Ambrose Church.

The Big Club Hall was originally named the North Italian-American Mercantile Company. It was organized in 1913 by northern Italian immigrants who came primarily from Lombardy.

It was first begun as a co-op where groceries could be purchased at a fair price. Stocks were sold to men only from northern Italy which were transferred to their eldest son. However, differences between north and south soon disappeared and it expanded into a social club. It became known as the Big Club Hall, a type of community center open to all Italians living on the Hill.

Political rallies, dances, and elaborate wedding celebrations were held here. It was a popular place where men would come together to play cards, enjoy a glass of wine, or simply sit around and share memories of the old country.

Time Moves On | HISTORY

Top Left: Big Club Hall's wedding cooks.
Top Right: Young ladies who served wedding guests at the Big Club Hall.

"Big Club Hall was 'the place' for wedding receptions. Often young men dropped in (uninvited) to enjoy the music and the food. No one seemed to mind!"

Friends and relatives enjoy a chicken and ravioli wedding feast.

RAVARINO AND FRESCHI, INC.

Joe Freschi and John Ravarino came to America in the late 1890s. In 1901, their first venture was manufacturing salami in a little store on 14th Street. They opened a grocery store on 19th Street, selling olive oil, cheese, pasta, rare wines, and liquor–all imported from Italy.

In 1916, with foresight and sound business sense, they purchased a lot on the corner of Kingshighway Boulevard and Shaw Avenue. Here they erected a three-story, fireproof, concrete building which became one of the largest production centers for macaroni products in the United States.

Both Ravarino and Freschi became American citizens in the year 1900. They were also members of the local Chamber of Commerce, the Rotary Club, and several non-profit organizations which provided mutual aid to Italian immigrants. These two men gave something beyond employment to the Hill. They upheld the tradition of honoring their Italian heritage while, at the same time, remembering their civic and patriotic duties as Americans.

The Ravarino and Freschi (R&F) plant on Kingshighway.

The Blackmer & Post Pipe Company

Time Moves On | HISTORY

SMOKESTACKS AND HARD LABOR

McQuay Norris Manufacturing Company

In 1919, McQuay Norris relocated to the Hill. Up until 1922, the company manufactured and sold piston rings exclusively. Male and female laborers found working conditions at the plant to be both safe and convenient. Since the factory was in their neighborhood, employees from the Hill had a short commute to work. This situation naturally reinforced the notion that the Hill community could eventually become entirely self-sufficient.

Quick Meal Stove Company (Magic Chef)

The Quick Meal Stove Company opened for business on the Hill in 1910. In the 1920s and 1930s, the company employed more than a hundred workers from the neighborhood. They were hired to build kitchen appliances such as range ovens. Working at Quick Meal was convenient for the residents of the Hill since it was only a short walk away from home. Once again, this strengthened the tradition of families not leaving the neighborhood.

Blackmer & Post Pipe Company

The Blackmer & Post Pipe Company was founded by Lucian Blackmer. In 1892, he built an expansive manufacturing operation, extending from Southwest Avenue to Arsenal Street. The company produced sewer and culvert pipes, as well as performing the function of adding glazed, clay cooping to protect the tops of brick walls. Later, the company began manufacturing septic tanks. The Blackmer & Post Pipe Company employed many Hill residents.

The Hill contained more than residential homes and small, family businesses. Large industries also occupied the region. These commercial institutions provided the residents with gainful employment. Although the work was difficult, the hours long, and the conditions sometimes unsafe, they did supply needed income.

LA BUON MARCA (A GOOD PRICE)

Many small businesses emerged on the Hill in the early 1900s. While they are almost too numerous to name, several are extremely notable. One such establishment was Rau Store, a dry goods store which was owned and operated by Phil Rau and his family. Local women never referred to it as the Rau Store. They coined it **"La Buon Marca"** which was a combination of Italian and English, meaning "A Good Price."

Berra's Dry Goods Store, run by Tony Berra, sold everything and anything that was remotely related to dry goods which, oddly enough, included candy! Stores like these meant more than mere transactions. It was here the ladies would meet, compare prices, and perhaps share a bit of local gossip—all in Italian.

Berra's Furniture Store was owned by John Berra and Louis Cerutti. Credit was never denied to anyone from the Hill. The owners had a unique way of keeping records. As a matter of trust, customers were given small ledger books and, every time a payment was made, it was simply subtracted from the total sale amount! They could pay once a week, once a month, or whenever they were able to.

Fair Mercantile Company, another early furniture store, was owned and operated by Mr. Paul and his sons. In the early 1900s, Mr. Paul originally peddled his wares out of two suitcases. He started out selling dry goods from house to house. Later, he purchased property on Shaw Avenue where he built a thriving furniture company, naming it the Fair Mercantile Company.

El's Drugstore, located on the 5100 block of Shaw, was where children delighted in buying penny candy. "Whenever I had to pick up my father's medicine, I always bought some candy. Mr. El never hurried me. He had so many choices." On Marconi, the Excel Drugstore and the adjoining Ice Cream Parlor was a popular meeting place for teenagers, where courtships could flourish over a strawberry sundae or a to-die-for chocolate malt.

Riggio Real Estate and Travel Agency in 1910.

Time Moves On | HISTORY

Left: Giuseppe and Santa Rumbolo came from Casteltermini, Agrigento, Sicily. Giuseppe was in the ice and coal business before he decided to become a grocer in 1948. Santa (photo) worked at the store's check-out counter. She knew every customer by name since they were more like friends to her. For nearly four decades, Rumbolo's became a part of every family they served.

"At one time, the Hill was dotted with grocery stores like Iovaldi's and Simontacchi's on Pattison; the Italian Co-op on Shaw; Leotta's on Daggett; Fassi's on Sublette; Rumbolo's on Shaw; Gioia's on Macklind; and Garavaglia's on the corner of Pattison and Marconi. Each store had its own unique character."

Ignazio, Joseph, and Frank Riggio, three brothers from Palermo, Sicily, left an indelible mark of community service on the Hill. As early as 1906, Ignazio and Joseph started a hardware store on the 5100 block of Shaw. Seeking to delve into other areas, they turned the business over to Frank. Ignazio and Joseph expanded into the foreign currency business, which was a vital function for a large number of Italian immigrants. Further ventures led them into real estate, insurance, and travel.

"The Riggios took care of my people's needs. When they arrived in Saint Louis, they needed a house, money, and insurance. They gave them more than assistance; they gave them confidence."

In 1948, Pope Pius XII recognized the dedication of Ignazio by honoring him with the Gold Cross of the Lateran, one of the highest awards a Catholic layman can receive. Mrs. Anna Riggio, who also excelled in humanitarian and Christian charities, was knighted in 1969 with the Gran Dama di Grazia, the highest award a Catholic laywoman can receive.

Center: Joseph Riggio, owner of Riggio Real Estate and Travel Agency.

Right: Ignazio Riggio.

Riggio Bank, on the corner of Shaw and Marconi. Today, Shaw's Coffee Ltd. occupies the space.

HISTORY | *Time Moves On*

After emigrating from Borgetto, Milan, Italy, John Volpi undertook the business of manufacturing Italian salami and sausage. He began on the corner of Daggett and Edwards (below) where he introduced his famous "Splendor Brand," which become an instant favorite. His salami was made only under his direct supervision. A century later, Volpi's is owned and operated by John's nephew, Armando Passetti, on the very corner it began. It continues to be a landmark for quality salami and sausage, known throughout the United States, Europe, and the Far East.

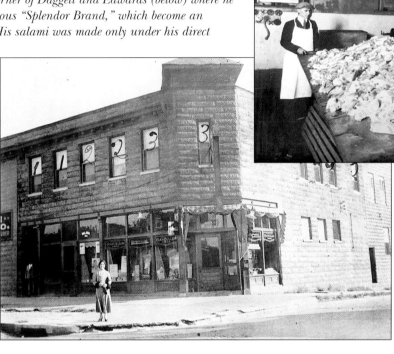

John Volpi (center of photo) and employees prepare Italian sausages (salami) in the Volpi plant. Huge salamis hang from the ceiling to dry.

John Colombo and Alessandro Fontana exchange the latest Hill news with a customer in Fontana's Market.

(L-R) Louis Merlo, Alessandro Fontana, and Martin Colombo stand outside Fontana's Market.

Time Moves On | HISTORY

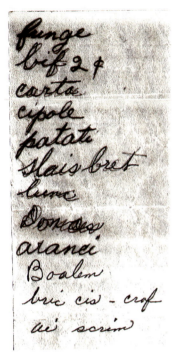

An Italian-American grocery list, circa 1902.

- Mushrooms
- Beef 2¢
- Paper
- Onions
- Potatoes
- Sliced Bread
- Lunch Meat
- Doughnuts
- Oranges
- Boiled Ham
- Brick Cheese/Kraft
- Ice Cream

John Viviano arrived in Saint Louis from Palermo, Sicily in 1924. He worked with his uncle who operated a macaroni factory downtown. Throughout his workday, Mr. Viviano would always dream about having his own business. With the support and encouragement of his friends, he saved and borrowed enough money to open a store (photo left) on the Hill in 1950. It soon became a successful family affair. Now, more than a half century later, John Viviano & Sons continues to run a brisk wholesale and retail operation which serves patrons throughout St. Louis and Illinois.

John and his wife, Angela, celebrate their 50th wedding anniversary in the photo below.

Gioia's Store opened for business in 1918. Chollie Gioia bought the store from Mr. Pellegrini, who was drafted during World War I. Every member of the Gioia family worked: the boys (Steve, Mike, and John) helped in the store, and the girls (Antoinette and Mary) helped their mother with chores.

But Gioia's was much more than a grocery store. It was where women went to buy necessary items, to chat, and to have a good-natured argument with Chollie. They would even go to the store to use his phone, since it was one of the few which existed in the neighborhood at the time. In the early days, Gioia's used to deliver groceries with a horse and buggy. Mike Merlotti, Steve Gioia, and John Gioia help with deliveries in the photo at right.

"We were so poor that we rarely had cash. Chollie gave us, and a lot of his customers, a credit book. When we bought something, he wrote the amount in 'The Book.' When we paid him at the end of the month, he would subtract the amount. Chollie always told us to just pay him whatever and whenever we could."

HISTORY | *Time Moves On*

THE STAFF OF LIFE

For every Italian, bread is the staff of life. Freshly baked bread is a natural part of every meal. Eating a piece of sliced bread from a local grocery store was somewhat of a novelty, with many families baking their own bread simply because it was the most economical thing to do. However, the Hill was replete with wonderful bakeries. As early as 1925, Carlo Baroli, nicknamed "Rebon" because he was born in Rubone, Italy, started his bakery in the basement of his home located on the 1900 block of Macklind. Daily, he delivered fresh, crusty loaves of bread in a hand pushcart, singing arias from his favorite operas as he made his morning deliveries.

Louis Amighetti opened the Amighetti Bakery in 1921. Working together with his son, they would bake from 4 A.M. to 5:30 P.M., five days a week. They used a mixture purchased by Louis, Sr. in 1928. Their oven operated using its original brick floor. At first, the oven was heated by wood but was later converted to gas. Ten-foot long wooden paddles were used to remove the bread from the oven. In 1969, the bakery was converted to a sandwich shop using only Amighetti Bakery bread. Today, under new ownership, it continues to be a popular bakery and deli.

Steve Gambaro and his brothers-in-law, Eugene and Frank Arpiani, were the original owners of the Missouri Baking Company. They first developed their craft in a bakery they owned and operated in Hackensack, New Jersey. In 1925, they built a bakery on Edwards Street, where they have continued to this day. Also in the 1920s, their relative, Ben Garavelli, opened a restaurant on Olive Street, offering his patrons fresh bread and pastries from Missouri Baking. The owners' original intent was to be exclusively a wholesale outlet. However, when wonderful aromas invaded the Hill neighborhood, there was an immediate demand for their products. Shortly after,

Missouri Baking Company in the 1920s.

Time Moves On | HISTORY

it became a retail operation for the entire Saint Louis community. In 1943, the Gambaro brothers and their sister, Joanne Gambaro-Arpiani, received ownership. In 1987, the bakery's reins were turned over to Mimi Gambaro-Lardo and Chris Gambaro. Once a simple corner retail store, the Missouri Baking Company has grown in popularity, drawing clientele from across the Midwest.

The Fazio Bakery has been operating on the Hill for over a century. Vincenzo DeMare purchased the bakery in 1902. The former owner was willing to sell when hoodlums, who wanted a share of his profits, threatened him. Not wanting any trouble, he sold the bakery. After DeMare bought the business, the hoodlums returned and threatened DeMare and family with harm if he did not comply with their demands. DeMare sent his family back to Italy and confronted the thugs, defying them with undaunted courage and the strength of his character. They immediately withdrew their threats.

In 1924, DeMare heard that Joe and Ben Fazio, fishermen from Sandusky, Ohio, were excellent workers so he offered Joe a job. When DeMare passed

Louis Amighetti, Jr. removes freshly baked bread from his bakery's huge oven.

Joanne Gambaro-Arpiani smiles as she waits on a young customer in this 1950s photo.

HISTORY | Time Moves On

away in 1926, Joe Fazio, who had since become DeMare's son-in-law, took over the business and eventually built the current bakery on Elizabeth Avenue. Joe's brother, Ben, joined him in 1929, until he went into business for himself in 1941. Charles, Joe Fazio's son, eventually followed in his father's footsteps.

"I helped my father, Joe Fazio, from the time I was a little boy. I made deliveries, house to house, when I was only eight years old, starting each day at 3 a.m. When I was only thirteen years old, I drove the bread truck to make deliveries. I never wanted to be a baker, so when I got married and began a family, I solicited business for my father. He gave me $2 for each customer I brought in! Finally, I suggested trying my hand at running the business for one year. Well, that was in 1961." It has now become a fourth-generation family business which continues to follow the basic lessons learned from their grandfather. They employ old-fashioned methods with updated machinery. They bake over 10,000 loaves of bread a day and over 7,000 buns. The fact that their production has increased dramatically attests to the demands for their quality product. Today, the Fazio Bakery is a wholesale bakery, a great inheritance from two men of noble character—Vincenzo DeMare and Joseph Fazio.

Past bakeries which also serviced the Hill were Gentile's and Fuse's Bakeries.

Joe Fazio proudly displays bread from his bakery.

Joe and Ben Fazio playfully duel with loaves of bread in front of the Fazio Bakery.

Members of the Fazio family step outside their bakery to enjoy a summer's day.

Time Moves On | HISTORY

Realizing the Hill was a good market for a soda-bottling firm, Isadore Oldani and Louis Venegoni formed the Blue Ridge Bottling Company at 2300 Brannon in 1914. They washed bottles, mixed the soda, filled the bottles, and then delivered the cases with a horse and buggy. In 1916, they moved to Shaw and Edwards. In 1921, they built a new plant at Kingshighway and Shaw. As the business grew, the five Oldani children and three Venegoni sons helped their fathers. The business prospered and flourished. By 1950, the firm, which began with two owners using a horse and buggy, grew to twenty trucks, fifty employees, and a state-of-the-art bottling factory. Blue Ridge Bottling Company, one of the Hill's former businesses, certainly attests to the area's work ethic, displayed by two great Italian immigrants–Oldani and Venegoni.

Young Italian immigrants dig ditches with picks and shovels in 1926. In the photo (L-R) are Frank Berra, Ernest Garavaglia, Alessandro Garavaglia, and Joseph Berra. These laborers' sons learned a great lesson from their fathers, who insisted they "go to school and get an education." Their sons followed their advice and became successful engineers, businessmen, and, more importantly, outstanding citizens of the Hill. It may be noted that the men are not related; these are common Italian names.

Louis Venegoni and Isadore Oldani inspect production at their Blue Ridge Bottling Plant.

Trucks loaded with cases of soda line up in front of the Blue Ridge Bottling Plant.

HISTORY | *Time Moves On*

TAVERNS

Men of the Hill know that many great tales are told over a glass of beer. Seen here in the 1920s are (Seated, L-R) Vito Moceri, Giuseppe "Joe" Anselmo, and Joe Dinatale. Standing are Pete Moceri, unknown, and Frank Distefiano.

Taverns dotted almost every corner on the Hill as they were rather exceptional places of business. They certainly did not depict the common image of a "saloon." Rather, they were more like social clubs. They were places to meet friends, exchange the latest news, enter a card game, or play a game of bocce. It was not uncommon to have bocce courts alongside or behind taverns.

As early as 1910, one of the most frequented taverns was Joe Ariotto's on Marconi. Joe Ariotto was a musician who also conducted a band. Patrons at Ariotto's tavern knew that an evening of music, friendship, and an occasional glass of wine would lift their spirits after a hard week's work in a clay mine.

Frank Gianella's tavern on Pattison was known as "Papa Prost." The name Papa Prost came from an interesting source. "Prost" is a German word for good luck or cheers. When Gianella's son, Paul, would enter the tavern calling out "Papa," the German patrons would laugh and answer "Prost!" and the name Papa Prost was born. Even though it was a drinking establishment, the neighborhood children were always welcome.

"As a child in 1923, all of us kids would go to Papa Prost. He had an old candy case and he would let us take all our time to pick out what penny candy we wanted. He even sold nickel grab bags. His was the only tavern which sold ice cream."

Another very unique tavern was Merlo's on the corner of Wilson and Marconi. Everyone called him "Forchet" which means fork in the northern dialect. It is believed that he was a farmer in Italy and pitched hay using a fork, hence the name. Whenever the twelve o'clock or the six o'clock evening church bells would ring, everything stopped and Mr. Merlo would not serve anyone. Respectful of the Church, he was a pious owner, requiring the men to be still while they prayed the Angelus!

In the 1930s, Giuseppe and Maria Spezia opened a little tavern called "Spezia's." It was located on the corner of

Above: Albino Pozza gets ready to saddle his horses to a wagon for his weekly trip downtown to buy supplies.

Albino Pozza in his tavern, which was later known as the "Seven Steps Tavern."

HISTORY *Time Moves On*

Daggett and Edwards Street. Later, Giuseppe's son-in-law, Charles Grassi, received ownership and it became "Charlie's Place, Acme of the World." When Charles Grassi and John Puricelli became partners, it was called "John and Charles." After Charles Grassi's death, it became "John and Rose's Place" until Puricelli's death, when it was simply named "Rose's" until it was sold in 1972. Multiple owners for more than half a century brought many changes, but Spezia's Tavern ultimately remained unchanged. The men of the Hill still sat around the tables and played cards. Hill children still bought little buckets of draft beer back home for their fathers.

"It was almost a ritual. When we were kids, my father would send me to buy a bucket of beer from Spezia's. It was every kid's goal to be able to swing the bucket around real fast and not spill a drop of beer. It didn't always work for me and my father wouldn't be too happy to get a bucket that was only half full. Fathers would get home from work around five o'clock. Before supper was ready, the kids high-tailed it to Spezia's to get a bucket of draft beer so it would be there for suppertime. There was a time when Spezia's even sold ice-cream."

The bocce courts behind the tavern drew men of the Hill, both young and old. The game was a source of wholesome competition, so everyone won. What someone lost in points, was gained in close-knit camaraderie.

One might feel they were caught in a time warp when first entering the Seven

The Italian Veterans Drum and Bugle Corps march on Marconi Street in front of Merlo's (Forchet's) Tavern.

(L-R) Charles Grassi and partner John Puricelli prepare drinks for customers in their tavern, named John and Charles at the time of the photo.

Time Moves On | HISTORY

Steps Tavern. It housed a large, sturdy, ornately carved bar. Behind the bar was an oval-topped, old-fashioned radio. The sizable cash register was over one hundred years old. A majestic, pot-bellied stove, built in the late 1800s, dominated the center of the room. Amazingly, this is how the tavern remained well into the 1980s. The tavern was operated by Regina Pozza, who came to America in 1919. She married Albino Pozza at St. Ambrose Church when it was still a small, wooden-frame church. Regina was quick to tell anyone who asked how she was able to run her business alone after the death of her husband: *"Life goes on—do no wrong, and no harm will come to you. Trust! We must trust one another!"*

Today, the Seven Steps Tavern has been razed and replaced by a parking lot. But the spirit of Regina's courage, trust, and love is a testament to the early Italian female immigrants.

Regina Pozza smiles as she greets her customers in her tavern at Shaw and Edwards.

Card games would inevitably start up when men gathered together in local taverns. Seated (L-R) are Mel Mercurio, "Bella," Elio Corso, and Sam DiGregario. Watching the action (L-R) are Tony Ribaudo, John Berra, and Yogi Berra.

The Seven Steps Tavern at Shaw and Edwards was built in 1888. Originally named "Pozza's," it was later changed to "Regina's."

HISTORY | *Time Moves On*

Joe "Ice" Ponciroli, owner of the Melrose Tavern, admires the Anheuser-Busch Clydesdale horses.

"Almost every corner on the Hill had a tavern. These taverns were family owned and served as a local meeting place. Men could have a drink after a long day of work or play a game of 'morra,' a nonbetting contest of strategy between two men. As the game involves the use of several hand gestures, it might look, only to an outsider, like the children's game 'rock, paper, scissors.'"

In 1957, John Riganti and Lou Aiazzi formed a partnership to open a new restaurant, hence the name "Rigazzi's." After several years, Riganti left to pursue other interests. Aiazzi, seeking to find a gimmick to attract customers, found a big fishbowl in a friend's basement. Recognizing that it was from the World's Fair, he took it to the restaurant and filled it with beer. It was an immediate success, and Rigazzi's is now famous for its "frozen fishbowls." At one time, the restaurant was the biggest seller of Budweiser beer in the entire state, so Clydesdales would periodically be sent to "visit" Rigazzi's.

In 2000, a devastating fire gutted the restaurant's interior but left the outer bricks intact. The building is over a hundred years old but continues to serve its customers as "Rigazzi's—Home of the Frozen Fishbowl." It is a warm and friendly place which typically draws huge crowds.

In the photo (L-R) are Louis Aiazzi, Martin Colombo, and John Riganti.

Time Moves On | HISTORY

The Call to Duty

World War I gave the Hill immigrants a special opportunity to prove their patriotism to America. A few men were recalled to Italy to serve, having previously signed up as reservists, but a larger number joined the American forces. They proudly pledged their allegiance and gratefully accepted American citizenship.

In the next generation, their sons were also proud of their country and, like their fathers before them, they would let the world know they were Americans, first and foremost.

There were 1,027 World War II servicemen from the Hill. A bronze plaque behind St. Ambrose is a somber reminder of the 23 young men from the parish who gave their lives for their country. Twelve more were prisoners of war and 49 were wounded in battle. After many tours of duty, they were awarded Bronze Stars, Distinguished Service Crosses, Purple Hearts, and Good Conduct Medals.

Reverend Charles Koester saw the need to keep the Hill boys in touch with their neighborhood. He initiated the publication of a newsletter called the *Crusader Clarion* which was sent to every Hill serviceman. Today, World War II veterans continue to praise Father Koester as he kept them from becoming homesick. Many of these young men had never ventured far from the Hill, and now they

Top: In 1916, Pete Valli served America during World War I.

Far left: Joseph Chiodini proudly served in the U.S. Army.

Center: Antonio Romano served in the U.S. Army during World War I.

Right: Gus Buttice proudly served in World War I.

found themselves oceans away from their loved ones. Despite the hardships they endured, they wrote letters filled with accounts of positive experiences.

"I never wanted my mom to worry about me. I knew that war was hell, but why give my mother more sadness?"

"While we were stationed in Nuremberg, Germany, I suggested to three of my buddies to go into Hitler's Black Forest and bring back some deer meat for supper. They shot and brought back three nice deer. We baked them in the oven and the battalion loved it. They tasted even better knowing we had robbed three prize deer from Hitler!"

"My brother spent three years in the Asiatic-Pacific Theatre. He was given a special assignment as a bricklayer, building machine-gun lookout towers because his civilian job had been with Laclede-Christy. This amused him since his job back home wasn't as a bricklayer. His commanding officer was so pleased with his work, he offered my brother a job to stay in Hawaii when the war was over. He turned it down because he was anxious to get home."

"My brother was in the Battle of the Bulge. He was shot and captured by the Germans. He spoke of a makeshift hospital that had been a schoolhouse at one time. There were no medical supplies, no gauze, only crepe paper. He told us how he had to care for his own gunshot wounds. Periodically, the women of the town would be marched through the aisles, spitting on the wounded

Top left: Anthony Ferrario shares happy moments with his wife, Annie, and children, Joe and Elizabeth, while he is on leave from the U.S. Army.

Above: Dominic Marfisi poses with Carl Colombo, the son of a family friend, before going overseas to Europe.

Left: Ermanno Imo (center) celebrates with friends after joining the Italian Army to work with Americans after the occupation.

Right: Antoinette "Toni" Gioia-Argentine served America in World War II as a W.A.A.C.

American soldiers. When we received news that he was missing in action, we gave him up for dead. But my mother would never let us believe that he was gone. She would say, 'God is good. He will send my son back!' He was liberated by the British and returned home."

"A friend of mine was only 22 years old when Uncle Sam called him. He was put in the Medical Corps and served in the South Pacific. I asked him how he could hold up after seeing so much human suffering. He only said, 'It was my duty to serve my country in any way I could. I never questioned otherwise.'"

Hill boys also fought in the Korean and Vietnam Wars. They fought despite the fact they didn't always feel the wars

Hugo Baldesi rests on an artillery shell while aboard ship.

Top right: John Anselmo returns home to his wife, Margaret, and his daughter, Maria. In World War II, he was injured by a land mine in Africa in 1944.

Left: Angelo and Lance Berra visit family while on furlough, after Angelo's release from a German prison.

Right: Mr. and Mrs. Tornetto and family visit their son, Larry, at Scott Air Force Base. He was recuperating from wounds received during the Korean War.

were justified. They were the sons of immigrants who were proud to be American, so they were fighting for their country. As loyal patriots, they understood the words of Henry Cabot Lodge: "Let every man honor and love the land of his birth, and the race from which he springs, and keep their memory green. It is a pious and honorable duty, but let us all be Americans."

But it was World War II which caused the greatest change on the Hill as it was no longer a neighborhood in isolation. Social and economic transitions were the result of conflicts in education, military life, and culture. Women began working in defense plants and became less sheltered, meeting men with different ethnic backgrounds. They became more mobile and were given greater opportunities for advancing their education.

The period following the war was essentially a period of assimilation. Cultural, occupational, and territorial boundaries began to disappear.

Yet, throughout all the changes, the Hill has retained many of the traditions which make it unique. It has grown a new image, but its foundation is its citizens, the sons and daughters of immigrants. People with a strong work ethic, a solid faith in their God, and in each other. Proud of their heritage, they are still ready to show the world that they are Americans.

Behind the Big Club Hall's bar are Nick Mazzola, Red Grassi, Gene Calcaterra, Midge Berra, Charles Iovaldi, and Paul Berra, Sr. who join their friends in celebrating the end of World War II.
Below: Charles Grassi and men from the Hill celebrate Italy's surrender in 1943.

Time Moves On | HISTORY

LIFE ON THE HILL

"There were no strangers. Everyone knew not only their neighbors, but everyone on the Hill. Neighbors helped neighbors. Children played in the streets. Life was uncomplicated. The children were safe. And that is what the Hill had more than anything else–children!"

"My mother made us roller-skate on the sidewalk, but it was more fun skating on the street! We only did it once, but my aunt saw us and she told my mother. You couldn't get away with anything since everybody told on you. Now I understand how right they were, but we certainly didn't appreciate it when we were kids!"

Josephine DiGregorio enjoys a relaxed moment at her home on Edwards Street.

Paul Torno strolls down Edwards carrying freshly baked bread.

79

HISTORY *Time Moves On*

BARBERSHOPS

Early barbershops on the Hill could very well be likened to England's 18th century coffee houses where philosophers, historians, wise men, heroes, and orators gathered. They, too, like the writers and intellects of the 18th century would hold debates over the latest political fiasco. Their friendly banter would give rise to hearty laughter, and tales of their heroism during battle were relived. In local barbershops, the men came not only to get a fifteen-cent haircut or a twenty-five-cent shave, but for more important reasons. It was where they could converse in their native tongue or enjoy a lively debate.

Barbershops, like the British coffee houses, were readily available. As early as 1928, several barbers serviced the Hill. There was Jake Cunetto on the 5000 block of Shaw; Sam Lusitano on the 5100 block of Shaw; Carlo on Edwards Street; Migo on Marconi (for some reason, no one could remember any of the barbers' last names); and Rancilio's shop which was adjoining the Big Club Hall on Marconi.

They were meeting places for an opportunity to philosophize, to argue, to boast, and, more importantly, they were a place where friends could relax and enjoy the richness of their camaraderie.

Little Dolores Caroli sits in her backyard on Shaw Avenue. The arena on Oakland Avenue can be seen in the background. The domed sports arena was razed in 1999.

In 1949, drying clothes in the sun was a common sight on the Hill. Left: Edith Garavaglia takes advantage of a sunny wash day.

Grandma Nunzi teaches her grandson, Charlie Gitto, Jr., how to dry tomatoes in the sun for making sauce.

Time Moves On | HISTORY

The Pozzos enjoy their backyard pond. Macklind Field is in the background.

"Macklind Field was an open field where Hill children held their baseball and soccer games. There were no bleacher seats, no benches, but their games drew large crowds from the neighborhood."

The Tunesi, Bartoni, Amighetti, and Miriani families enjoy a backyard picnic.

Alessandro Fontana pours a glass of wine for relatives sitting around his kitchen table.

81

THE FRONT PORCH

Prior to the comforts of the modern air conditioner, Hill residents used their front porches. It was where friends would meet, sit, and share the latest gossip; or where they sat quietly to read a book or the newspaper. As everyone sat on his or her front porch in the early evening, they were sure to be greeted by someone in the neighborhood, even if only to stop for a few moments to share the latest news or to laugh at a joke. While air conditioning provides an escape from St. Louis' hot, humid days, it may have deprived communities of the wonderful feeling of communicating with one's neighbors. This is not the case on the Hill. People still watch the world go by as they relax on their front porches.

Front porches line Shaw Avenue.

David "Butchie" Fontana wears his favorite sailor's shirt.

Time Moves On | HISTORY

Left: Dolores Berra and her bridesmaids leave for St. Ambrose Church.

Right: Bill Mack stops to chat with Louis Ceriotti, the gentleman relaxing on the front steps.

Bottom Left: (L-R) Rose Fontana-Kelso, Nazarene Fontana, and Gloria Fontana-Gambaro sit on their front porch waiting for their friends to join them.

Bottom Right: (L-R) Fannie Berra, Marie Carnaghi, Linda Pozza, and Rose Stratton have an enjoyable visit while sitting on Fannie's porch.

HISTORY
Time Moves On

GARDENS

(l-r) "Rick" and Joe Lange enjoy an afternoon hunting for mushrooms.

Albert Camus once wrote, "In the depths of winter, I finally learned that within me, there lay an invincible summer." His message of hope for things to come is perhaps what gardens were for the early Hill people. In preparation for the summer's crop, they held the promise for a plentiful harvest.

When they planted in the spring, they looked forward to great tomato plants, eggplants, green peppers, lettuce, and even Swiss chard. These vegetables would enable them not only to feed their families, but also to help save on food bills.

Every garden contained wonderful, aromatic herbs such as parsley, mint, and basil. The amazing part is that these household Italian cooks were able to take an ordinary garden vegetable and turn it into something our modern-day society would consider a gourmet dish. Gardens, indeed, were a thing of hope, almost a religious experience. They were looked upon and tended with a loving care.

"When I was a kid at St. Ambrose School, we would walk in a procession behind the priest while he blessed every garden on the Hill. I think they were called Rogation Days. He was asking God to bless the gardens so, in the summer, the plants would yield good vegetables."

Despite the harshness of winter and the difficulties life would inevitably bring, what these families could grow in their own backyard became a way of expressing that "invincible summer" which lives in all of us.

Mrs. Mary Russo tends to her backyard garden.

In 1941, students from the Henry Shaw School weed their Victory Garden.

GRANDPAS

Louis Berra delights in seeing his granddaughter, Anna, enjoy her very first taste of ice cream.

Giuseppe Ceriotti carries granddaughter, Patricia Merlo, in the backyard for a stroll.

Martin Garavaglia listens closely as his granddaughter, Sally, whispers her secrets in his ear.

In Italian families, grandfathers are held in the highest regards as their beloved and respected patriarchs. The first born grandchild is traditionally named after their paternal grandfather. Children are taught to greet their nonno (grandfather) with a hug and kiss.

HISTORY | *Time Moves On*

CARS

Dominic LaFerla and his family prepare to take a ride.

(L-R) Louis Moroni, Joe Ceriotti, and Harry Ceriotti on Magnolia in the 1920s.

Standing in front of the Russo family's Deluxe Service Station in 1932 are Mrs. Nunzia Russo, holding her infant daughter, Anne, and standing next to her daughter, Tina.

Time Moves On | HISTORY

GIRLS

Top left: Adeline DiLiberto-Paulos (far left) and friends met every Sunday on Bischoff Avenue to ride their bikes, take a walk to Forest Park, or take in a movie.

Top right: (L-R) Angeline Mazzola, Judy Berra, Ann Oldani-Zarinelli, and Katie Miriani-Rossi enjoy a swim at a St. Ambrose Church picnic.

Bottom left: Seventeen-year-old Dora Foglia-Devoti, models her fur stole in the 1930s.

Bottom right: The 1947 Excel Drugstore Gang gather to enjoy a gelati (an Italian ice cream).

HISTORY | Time Moves On

Hawks, Ravens, Crusaders, Vikings, and More

When Italian immigrants first came to the Hill in the late 1800s, there was little or no time for indulging in pastimes. Working long hours allowed them neither the time nor the energy to play sports. However by 1925, the Hill's population had grown to over 5,000 occupants and a large number of its youth now had more free time for recreation. With their fathers better able to provide for them, it gave the children more opportunities to be involved in sporting activities.

"When we were kids we played anywhere–in open fields, backyards, and in empty lots. We didn't have any sophisticated electronic toys in the 1930s, like our kids have today. With a simple piece of clothesline, we would jump rope. Boys made scooters out of a single roller skate and an old orange crate. They even made their own hockey sticks. They played roller hockey on Boardman since it wasn't a busy street, and the cops wouldn't chase them off as much. Sometimes, we had to tie strings around a softball to keep the stuffing from falling out. But we always made do. We could never buy a ball. Who had any extra money? We would look for balls in the River Des Peres and sometimes we got lucky. We even put on marvelous plays for the neighborhood in our backyard, sometimes charging a penny for admission. We just made our own fun."

The Hill had plenty of places for young people to congregate, safe and sound. Hopeful young athletes could play or watch softball and soccer games at the Fairmount Playground on the corner of Boardman and Shaw. For neighborhood children, the Foundry Field at Kingshighway and Southwest or the Shaw School playground were some of the carefree locations their parents could find them after school. But when the bells of Saint Ambrose Church rang out at six, they had to hurry home before suppertime! Furthermore, when the

Mr. Paul Calcaterra (photo center, wearing suit and tie), funeral director on the Hill, sits with the baseball team he sponsored.

Liggett & Myers factory whistle blew its nine o'clock whistle, they instinctively knew it was time to literally run home. For every child, it was an unwritten law that they be home when this whistle blew.

It was in 1930 when Joe Causino, the athletic supervisor at the local Southside Y.M.C.A., recognized the need to form athletic clubs for boys. Uncle Joe, as he was affectionately called, provided them with the opportunity to play and swim at the Y.M.C.A. He knew their families had little or no money to pay for membership and, more importantly, he recognized the need to have a place to release all their unbounded, youthful energy. Through Causino's ambition and leadership, many young men were then able to channel their energy into more wholesome areas. As is the case today, when young men can stay out of trouble, they are able to fulfill their promise of never bringing shame to their families. They learned an important lesson from their parents that upholding their family's good name was truly one of the greatest achievements of their young lives.

"I guess I stayed out of trouble because I never wanted to hurt my mother. Plus, I had a healthy fear of disappointing my father."

In a short amount of time, there were more than 25 clubs on the Hill. Clubs with such names as: the Hawks, the Ravens, the Panthers, Alley Rats, Outlaws, the Royal Knights, Crusaders, Stags, Vikings, Orioles, Flats, and the Fawns became fine institutions which instilled pride and loyalty into the young men of the Hill. Today, many groups continue to meet, holding their membership as a badge of honor.

Meetings were sometimes held in basements, garages, sheds, and even in residential homes. For each club, elections would be held, activities planned, and sporting teams would be organized.

Above: The Macklind Athletic Club displays their trophy.

Left: Members of the Wildcat Athletic Club sit for a club picture in 1942. As a life lesson, the Hill's club coaches expected their teams to always be respectful towards others.

HISTORY *Time Moves On*

Primarily, they became athletic clubs competing in the two most popular sports on the Hill: baseball and, of course, soccer! These clubs, of which many were under the direction and guidance of Mr. Causino, would provide safe and wholesome activities for the Hill's youth.

Several young men attained national and even international acclaim. Among them are: professional baseball players Joe Garagiola and Yogi Berra. The five soccer players who were chosen from the Hill community to play on the United States World Cup team were Bob Annis, Frank Borghi, Charlie Colombo, Gino Pariani, and Frank Wallace. In Brazil, the U.S. team defeated England for the World Cup Championship in 1950. Still today, it is considered one of the biggest upsets in the history of the game. This was a thrilling accomplishment for five young men who had little more that their own dreams to propel them towards international fame. When they reached the height of notoriety, it was important that they never forget their roots. They were the sons of Italian immigrants, who knew that determination and hard work were essential ingredients for a successful life.

Charles Rossi (driver) cruises with his Crusader friends in his Uncle Jep's Model-T Ford. Dominic Italiano stands directly behind Charles (outside the car). The two young men (standing to the left of Charles) are (L-R) Frank Calcaterra and Nick Mazzola.

Time Moves On | HISTORY

Members of the Ravens Soccer Team played in the C.Y.C. Soccer League during the 1948-49 season.

Seen below is a New Year's Eve celebration given by the members of the Flats Club. The sign behind the group is a remnant of the previous month's dance on Thanksgiving Eve. The origin of the club's name was due to the fact that its members claimed to be "flat broke." Additionally, their clubhouse was housed in a flat at 5100 Daggett Avenue.

HISTORY | Time Moves On

AND GIRLS, TOO

Young ladies on the Hill were not to be outdone by their male counterparts. They, too, belonged to special clubs and organizations.

Members of the St. Ambrose Grail Club, founded by Monsignor Adrian Dwyer.

Young Marcalettes Girls Club, circa 1937. In order to become a member, one or more of their parents must have originated from Marcallo, Italy.

Time Moves On | HISTORY

Wives and friends of the Fawns Athletic Club meet to enjoy their Annual Dinner Party in 1951.

The Kittens, wives and girlfriends of the Wildcats, have a Mother-Daughter Party.

HISTORY | *Time Moves On*

BOCCE CLUB

The Hill immigrants have a long history in belonging to clubs. They have been members of social, athletic, and religious organizations. In keeping with this tradition and their love of the game of bocce, the Italia-America Bocce Club was formed. In 1975, the club was founded on Manchester Avenue. Its membership grew, and it became necessary to find a larger building. Members who were tradesmen and construction contractors volunteered their services to remodel the old McQuay Norris plant, while some of the other men remodeled the plant's shower room. The Italia-America Bocce Club has become a place for members to relax, meet with friends, and play a competitive game of bocce.

Left: Men from the Hill enjoy an afternoon playing on the bocce courts at Rose's Tavern.

The Italia-America Bocce Club currently occupies the former McQuay Norris Manufacturing Company plant.

Time Moves On | HISTORY

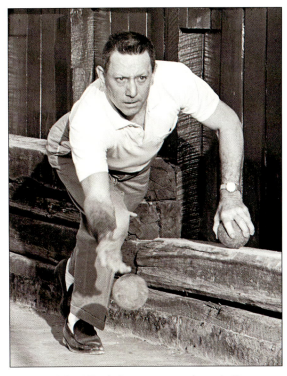
Celesti Zeni throws a mean bocce ball.

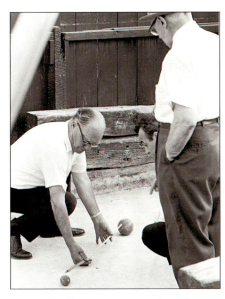
Joe Verdi measures on a close play.

Sam LaFerla prepares to score points for his bocce team.

Bocce is a game played by eight individuals in two teams with two from each team permanently stationed at either end of the court. Each frame consists of eight balls being thrown from one side of the court, with each player throwing two balls apiece. The court is rectangular with a short, narrow wall on its borders. A coin toss determines which team will go first and the color of balls for each team. The first team tosses out the target ball (pallino) which must cross the center line, but not hit the back wall. If the first team fails to land the pallino, a player from the second team tosses the pallino. The first player from the original (or first) team then throws the first ball. The object of the game is to get as close to the pallino as possible. After the second team makes its first attempt, the players alternate turns until all balls are thrown. Whenever a team gets a ball closer, it steps aside and lets the other team throw. Only one team scores in a frame. One point is given for each ball that is closer to the pallino than the closest ball of the opposing team.

At the end of the first frame, the balls are moved to the opposite end of the court and the contest continues from that end. Games are played to thirteen points, which normally amounts to twelve frames. Players may bank the ball off the side walls and may step on, but not over, the foul line before releasing the ball. A ball hitting the back wall is dead and must be removed unless it first hits another ball in which case all balls are valid.

Not only is it a national sport, the game is also played internationally. The Hill is proud to have Aldo Della Croce, Lou Salamone, and Julie Imo on the National U.S. Bocce Federation Board of Directors.

(L-R) Caesar Venegoni, Steve Gioia, Charles "Max" Berra, and Charles Piantanida get ready for the great rabbit feast in 1930.

In the early 1930s, Primo Canero (holding bread) is honored at a Big Club Hall Banquet as he was once the World Heavyweight Boxing Champion.

Time Moves On | HISTORY

The Hill's chapter of the Wapello Tribe #110

The Improved Order of Red Men is the oldest fraternal organization of purely American origin. It is a benevolent and charitable non-profit group whose foundations are patriotism, good fellowship, brotherhood, and mutual assistance. The Hill community's branch is known as the Wapello Tribe #110, and it was instituted in August of 1904.

Another important social and cultural club was La Pirandello. It was organized in 1938 by the youth of Sicilian immigrants, and named for the Sicilian dramatist, novelist, and Nobel Prize winner, Luigi Pirandello. It was the only club in the City of St. Louis which performed in the Sicilian dialect. Even though it was a dramatic club, it also functioned as a social organization, sponsoring occasional picnics and dances.

John Anselmo (second from right) and friends enjoy a game of pool in the 1940s.

97

HISTORY   *Time Moves On*

SOCCER

Soccer has always been the predominant sport in Italy. It is not surprising that the young sons of Italian immigrants have made this their favorite sport in America. One could make the argument that their dedication was partially responsible for St. Louis becoming a national center for the sport of soccer. Internationally, the preeminent goal is the quest for the World Cup. Strangely, this match against the powerful England team in the 1950 Cup games, which included four Hill residents, received little or no local media attention at the time.

Frank Borghi gets ready to block England from scoring during the World Cup Championship Game.

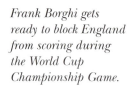

The Simpkins Soccer Team from the Hill. They won the U.S. Soccer Championship in 1948.

Time Moves On | HISTORY

BERRA, BUCK, AND GARAGIOLA

Joe Garagiola, Jack Buck, and Lawrence "Yogi" Berra have all received the honor of being in the Baseball Hall of Fame. At one time Joe, Jack, and Yogi all lived on the same block in the Hill neighborhood. Jack's daughter, Christine, recalls that "When I was a child, I thought our family's name was shortened to Buck from Buckanero since we lived in an Italian neighborhood."

Joe Garagiola hams it up for Yogi Berra (left) and the highly esteemed Joe DiMaggio (right).

Yogi Berra and Carmen celebrate their wedding in 1949.

Vince Cunetto (standing) looks on as Jack Buck, with daughter Julie on his knee, accepts an award at the Cunetto House of Pasta.

(L-R) Jack Buck and Joe Garagiola (both sitting) with another legendary sports announcer, Harry Caray (standing).

HISTORY | Time Moves On

Hill residents, both men and women, have participated in numerous sports including golf, bowling, tennis, and, of course, bocce! Church organizations from St. Ambrose have always supported various sports activities.

Ben Pucci played tackle in the N.F.L. for the Cleveland Browns.

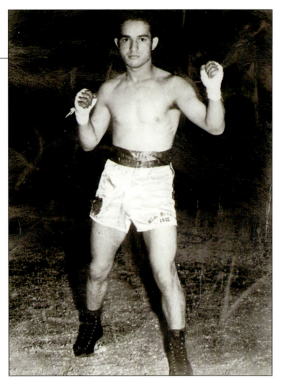

Golden Gloves Champion Joe DiMartino was a wholesome young athlete who made his immigrant parents proud.

Over the years, the Hill has produced some first-class athletes. A recent example is Jeff Cacciatore (#11) who plays forward for a professional soccer team, the Fort Lauderdale Strikers.

The St. Ambrose Holy Name Society sponsored this group of bowlers in 1953.

ENTERTAINMENT

The performing arts run deep in the soul of an Italian. To paraphrase Shakespeare, "Every 'Italian' is an actor, and the world is his or her stage."

The Vincenzo Bellini Drama Society, founded in 1910, was named after a noted opera composer. It played an important role in the cultural and artistic life of the Hill's early immigrants. It gave them the opportunity to not only view dramatic productions, but to encourage them to actively participate. The fact that they usually performed in Italian was an added benefit for those who did not speak English yet.

"On Sunday afternoons, my father and mother would take me to see a play by the Vincenzo Bellinis. It made my parents so happy since it was all in Italian. I guess that's where I learned to appreciate my Italian background."

Continuing the Hill's love of the arts by recognizing a young adult's passion for drama, Charles "Skip" Torretta, a talented musician and composer, wrote, produced, and directed shows in the 1940s. Early productions were presented in the basement of Saint Ambrose Church.

"Joe Ariotto was a strict disciplinarian. He would assign specific times for each student to practice at home. To make sure, he would walk by their house and, if they were not working on their next lesson, they would receive a sharp crack from his baton."

Joe Ariotto, the Hill's most popular musician in the 1930s, entertained in various functions which included playing for weddings, funerals, and church processions. He also taught music lessons to Hill youngsters. In the photo, Joe Ariotto's Famous Military Band prepares to entertain the residents of the Hill.

HISTORY | *Time Moves On*

Above: The Vincenzo Bellini Drama Society poses on stage at St. Ambrose Church.

Top Right: Frank Daniels grew up on the Hill and attended Henry Shaw School. In June of 1941, he wrote the Shaw School Theme Song. *After graduating from Southwest High School, he became a successful composer, lyricist, and music educator. His most popular hit,* My Heart Belongs To Only You, *was recorded by many artists including Bobby Vinton and Jackie Wilson.*

Right: At the local Henry Shaw School, members of the Glee Club are photographed in the 1950s.

ACCORDION

Almost every kid on the Hill learned how to play the accordion.

"My father loved the accordion. When he came home from work, the first thing he would say to my brother was, 'Did you practice today?' After supper, my brother would play for my father. I can still see him sitting and tapping his feet as my brother played. Today, we still tease my brother because he really didn't get past learning the song, *Lady of Spain*!"

Neighbors enjoyed hearing Ray Kercher practice his accordion in his front yard on Pattison Avenue.

A few notes from John Giacoma's accordion was all Ermanno Imo needed to burst out into song.

Rosemarie Restelli plays the accordion; her brother, Carl, the piano; and her father plays the mandolin.

THEATRES

By the early 1920s, the Hill's immigrants had become more financially stable. Therefore, they had more opportunities and time to pursue additional recreational arenas. Several theatres offered entertainment to the residents of the Hill. The Nickelodeon, located in an empty lot on the corner of Marconi and Daggett, showed silent movies in an open-air theatre. Families could also attend performances of old Italian folklore which were told by Mario Milano's string puppets. The Family Theatre, owned and operated by Giovanna Lange, opened on Shaw Avenue in 1915. Children would pay only a nickel for admission and, if they were fortunate enough to have another nickel, they would buy a grab-bag full of candy.

The Columbia Theatre, located at Southwest and Edwards Street, opened in 1925. It introduced talking films and vaudeville acts to the Hill residents. Children would fill the theatre for week-

Moviegoers line up for a matinee during the Holidays at the Columbia Theater in 1953.

end double features for an affordable ten-cent admission fee. Their parents had the comfort of knowing their children would be safe while enjoying some wholesome entertainment. Also, parents were particularly pleased since they knew the theatre's owner would make sure they remained well supervised.

"Nobody made any noise or fooled around during the Columbia show! We knew better because, if anyone got out of hand or acted up, the lights would go on and the movie would stop. And God help us if we put our arms around a girl. Bess Schulter's flashlight would shine right on us, and we would get the message real fast!"

Little Raymond Lange stands ready to enjoy a show at the Family Theatre on Shaw Avenue.

Gloria Fontana-Gambaro checks the coming attractions advertisement at the Columbia Theatre. Since the Columbia's closing, the theatre building underwent various transitions which included a racquetball center, an art studio, and a private residence.

(L-R) Dolores Restivo, Charlie Riva, and Lou Berra are seen leaving the Columbia Theatre after enjoying a 1947 movie, The Razors Edge, starring Tyrone Power and Gene Tierney.

HISTORY — *Time Moves On*

POLITICS

Left: Monsignor Lupo and members of the St. Ambrose Church Board are pictured in the early 1940s.

Below: Taking part in a meeting of the Hill's local political leaders are (L-R) Charles Iovaldi, Edith and Gene Calcaterra, Louis "Midge" Berra, Paul Berra, Tony Puricelli (sitting), and Tony Mascazzini.

Prior to the Great Depression, the Hill's 24th Ward was staunchly Republican. Meetings were held at Gioia's Hall, located at Edwards and Pattison, and Mr. Joe Gioia was the Hill's Republican leader.

However, during the Depression jobs were few and income almost non-existent. The Democratic Club, under the leadership of Louis "Gene" Gualdoni, soon became the political nucleus of the Hill. Gualdoni recognized the potential leadership ability in Louis "Midge" Berra and he introduced him to the political world. Unlike the politics of today, the Hill's version was much more personal. The Democratic Club, open every Friday night, was where Gualdoni and Berra would answer questions as well as help people resolve any difficulties they may have encountered. During tax season, they were open on Monday, Wednesday, and Friday nights and residents would have their tax returns completed at no cost. If anyone needed to pay a bill at City Hall, they could take their payment to the Democratic Club and their bills would be taken downtown for them.

It was in the 1940s when Eugene Mazzuca, under the tutelage of Midge Berra, became an integral part of the 24th Ward. It was not uncommon for Midge Berra to instruct Mazzuca to take food to a needy family or arrange to have coal delivered. The Club would often provide rental payments for a distressed family. However, the need for assistance was short-lived since families could easily find work when Midge Berra set his mind to it. But more importantly, these political leaders would help local immigrants obtain citizenship, which gave them a sense of identity. They were no longer outsiders, they were Americans. The political era of Midge Berra was one of commitment. A handshake with one of these political figures could be considered as binding support. When someone offered his or her hand, it meant his word and his trust. In Berra Park, a statue of Midge Berra symbolizes the true meaning of political leadership–trust, respect, and honor.

Today, with the language barrier all but disappeared, the times have changed as political views on the Hill have become more independent.

Below: The Hill mourns the passing of a great political leader, Louis "Midge" Berra.

HISTORY | *Time Moves On*

Waiters and bartenders gather to prepare for the evening's event at the Hill's former premiere nightclub, the Club Casino, located on the 5300 block of Wilson.

Right: Il Pensiero (The Thought), *an Italian newspaper, was established in 1904 under the direction of Dr. Cesare Avigni. Almost a century later, it continues today under the capable direction of Antonio Lombardo.* Il Pensiero *is the voice of the Italians, bringing both news and culture into the homes of the Hill. It is the only Italian newspaper published in the state of Missouri.*

Mrs. Rosalie Vicari-Sferlazza (seventh from the left) and her daughter, Connie Mary, join mothers with their young children for a celebration at the Public Health Clinic on Race Course Avenue in 1929.

Time Moves On | **HISTORY**

Southwest Bank of Saint Louis opened in October of 1920, in a building that had previously been a small tavern. On the Hill, the bank was, and still is, referred to as the Hill Bank. During the stock market crash of 1929, not a single customer lost any money. Mr. Freschi, one of the original owners of the R&F Spaghetti Factory, was a senior bank officer who could communicate with the Italian (or non-English speaking) customers. At the time of the crash, he encouraged them not to withdraw their deposits. Customers on the Hill were always faithful and understood that runs on the bank would certainly end in disaster. Because of customer loyalty, Southwest Bank was one of the few which survived the Great Depression without anyone losing a deposit.

On April 24, 1953, four men robbed the bank at gunpoint. Police foiled the robbery after receiving calls from telephone repairmen who were working out back at the time of the stick-up. In a shootout, one police officer was wounded and a second missed a shotgun blast to his head by only four inches. Two of the robbers were shot, a third took his own life rather than surrender, and the fourth robber escaped but was later captured. The cash was returned and counted. The bank ended up with more money as, evidently, the robbers lost some of their own currency. Based on these events, a movie was later produced–*The Great Saint Louis Bank Robbery* starring Steve McQueen.

Southwest Bank has grown tremendously, but it is still known locally as the Hill Bank. Why is this? Perhaps no one has ever forgotten or lost sight of the fact that, back in the 1920s, its loyal customers were responsible for building Southwest Bank into a solid institution which continues to grow.

The great robbery of Southwest Bank in 1953.

HISTORY | *Time Moves On*

After the Hill 2000 Celebration, Reverend Vincent Bommarito (on left, wearing Camp Richards T-shirt) cleans the church lot with young Hill people. This photo was taken when Reverend Bommarito was a seminary student.

THE CHURCH AND HER PEOPLE

To this day, St. Ambrose continues to be the nucleus of the Hill region. Almost all local activities tend to revolve around the Church. Out of love and loyalty to the people around them, parishioners become involved by serving the community in a variety of ways. With this central purpose in mind, both young and old have shared their free time as volunteers in numerous service projects. There is never any need for special invitations, as all are welcome to participate.

Taken in 1977, these dedicated women volunteered to clean the church once a week. Local parishioners have continued this tradition ever since.

Time Moves On | HISTORY

Leo Giuffrida, the custodian for the St. Ambrose School, was a class favorite, greeting every student by name. As a faithful servant, Leo rose above his personal disabilities, making him beloved by the entire parish.

After a formal wedding service at St. Ambrose Church, the festivities continued at the Big Club Hall. Pictured are the female servers for the Bossi-Pozzo wedding which took place in the 1940s.

Monsignor Salvatore Polizzi (far left) greets St. Ambrose parishioners following the unveiling of the Immigrant Statue in the 1970s.

History | *Time Moves On*

"When I was a child, my entire family marched in the Santa Rosalia Procession. It was a beautiful tradition. All of the young kids looked forward to the evening, when a wonderful fireworks display was given in honor of their Saint."

Standing at the front of their lines are (L-R) Jasper Lonigo and Mr. DeFiore. These men would take the lead as young men were about to carry the St. Rosalie statue through the Hill streets for her procession.

Priests, altar boys, and parishioners proceed through the Hill's streets for the Corpus Christi procession in 1979.

Time Moves On | HISTORY

In 1947, Sister Imelda's fourth-graders smile for their class picture.

"I attended St. Ambrose when Mussolini was Italy's dictator. We had textbooks with chapters praising his leadership. They even taught us songs about fascism, the rising glory of Italy, and all the wonderful deeds of 'Il Duce.' After discovering the truth about his regime, we now realize he was nothing more than a brutal enemy of the people. Looking back, I'm amazed at how quickly someone can fall from grace in the eyes of our community and the eyes of God."

In 1938, St. Ambrose students are honored in a graduation ceremony after completing a course in Italian studies.

HISTORY | *Time Moves On*

SACRED HEART VILLA

Sacred Heart Villa's Day Nursery.

The Villa children enjoy their noontime lunch.

Since 1939, the Sacred Heart Villa has continued to be an excellent day care center. It is a beautifully constructed building, but the institution is more than a brick and mortar structure–it is all heart! It revolves around Sister Felicetta Cola, who is all heart! Sister Felicetta came to the Villa in 1939, before the building was even completed. Barely five feet tall, she readily dispensed tot-level hugs with no difficulty at all. She kept her classes of three-year-olds busy with singing, stories, and playtime. Her theory was that to be happy, children needed love. They never passed by her without receiving a warm hug. In addition to teaching classes, Sister Felicetta taught piano lessons to children from kindergarten to eighth grade. In her spare time, her hobby was making pasta including fettuccini, angel hair, linguini, and lasagna. Always a hit at church bazaars, her pasta was also sold at local shops on the Hill. She is truly the heart of the Villa, having ministered to children for over half a century. Today, her health is fragile but her spirit is stable and strong.

Once a year, the Sisters held a Day of Recollection for the women of the parish. It was a day set aside to "slow down" and relax, away from the busy chores life can bring. It was a day to share some "now" time with God. Photo Right: The Christian Mother's Society is entertained with an afternoon movie in Italian.

Sister Felicetta entertains her pre-school children. Photo by Richard Finke.

"When I was a little girl, I took piano lessons from Sister Felicetta. She was a great teacher, and she taught me other things besides music. She taught me how to make homemade pasta. Every Saturday morning, I would go to the Villa to help Sister. However, I learned much more than how to make dough. Sister taught me patience, not to rush, and to enjoy the little things in life."

Restaurant Recipes

As part of the Hill experience, the food industry plays an important role in the community. With numerous bakeries, family markets, sandwich shops, wholesale outlets, and businesses which import Italian goods from Europe, this small neighborhood in St. Louis has consistently drawn clientele from across the globe. Despite its relative size, the Hill possesses some of the finest Italian restaurants in the country. Four of the best are Charlie Gitto's "On the Hill," Dominic's, Giovanni's, and Cunetto House of Pasta who have contributed some of their most popular dishes. A large majority of the following recipes were created by the chefs from each of these award-winning establishments. Even though their patrons have included nationally known figures and celebrities, guests will not only enjoy a great meal; they'll leave feeling like royalty themselves.

Charlie Gitto's

"Imagination is stronger than knowledge," Charlie Gitto quotes Einstein, and as the owner of the house that created toasted ravioli, he is in complete agreement. The first time he entered the restaurant he later bought, was when he was eight years old. At the time, his father was the maitre d' of Angelo's. Young Charlie worked every day after school foil-wrapping potatoes, cleaning behind the bar, and polishing the brass. He earned 75 cents a day.

"Angelo's was primarily a steakhouse so I learned to cook from my mother and grandmother." Gitto bought Angelo's from the latter's three sisters, Gina, Mary, and Teresa. "I've always loved this restaurant. It was my dream and my ambition to run and own it, especially since it's the place where toasted ravioli was born. This restaurant was not willed to me by my father, contrary to what many people think. I started from scratch and built." Initially, Gitto lived on the second story with his wife, Paula, and their four children.

Since Gitto took over Angelo's in 1981, other changes have taken place: he added a garden room, remodeled the kitchen, and expanded the dining area. The décor features more contemporary artwork. The large and bright dining room has an adjacent 8-table patio. Gitto caters to current trends such as the Atkins and South Beach diets. To this end, he has added menu items including high protein entrees and grilled vegetables. He also offers vegetarian and fusion choices, like San Francisco ciopino and pan-seared ahi tuna prepared Japanese style. The chef is similarly proud of his traditional "staples" such as cannelloni from the north and, tortellini a la panna (creamed) from the south.

The Tommy LaSorda room came into being when Gitto renovated in 1989. "I called up LaSorda and said, 'Tommy, you often bring in groups of 10 to 12, so can I name that new room after you?' Tommy is great. He talks to regulars, remembers names, and is personality plus." Other famous guests have included Joe DiMaggio, St. Louis' own Vincent Price, Ernest Borgnine, TV talk show host Merv Griffin, and "the very pleasant" Howard Cosell.

He enjoys a good relationship with his father, Charlie, Sr., who since 1974, has run a restaurant downtown with Charlie Junior's sister, Karen. His mother, Annie, is "officially retired" or "trying to be." His brother owns Johnny Gitto's in South St. Louis. Charlie's daughter, Amy, works in two restaurants in Philadelphia and Charlie Gitto, III studies at the University of Missouri. Charlie's daughter, Suzanne, troubleshoots at Dad's restaurant and his son, Anthony, is learning to cook. Charlie's wife, Paula, helps run the dining room.

"The Original" Toasted Ravioli

The fried, meat-filled pasta pillows served with a marinara sauce became a St. Louis original and a staple, much like the ice cream cone. Although there are many stories claiming this St. Louis treasure, Charlie declares, "Let there be no doubt this baby is credited to Charlie Gitto's 'On The Hill.'"

As a mistake-turned-clever-invention, a cook dropped some cooked ravioli in bread crumbs by accident. Rather than toss it out, he deep-fried it to a golden brown color. At Charlie Gitto's, they still make the original recipe in their kitchen. The following, however, is an easier version.

Ingredients
1 cup milk
1 large egg lightly beaten
2 cups dry Italian-seasoned bread crumbs
1 pkg. meat ravioli
2 qts. vegetable oil for frying
grated parmesan cheese
fresh tomato sauce

Combine milk and egg in a bowl, making an egg wash. Place bread crumbs in a separate bowl. Dip frozen ravioli in milk wash and coat with bread crumbs.

Place in hot oil (350 degrees). Fry ravioli until golden brown. Place on drainboard, sprinkle with parmesan cheese, and serve immediately with tomato sauce.

Serves 4

Charlie Gitto's | RECIPES

121

VEAL NUNZIO

"This dish was created in the early 1980s by my late brother, George "Nunzio" Gitto, and myself. We created the dish as an alternative to Veal Oscar. This dish can be made with chicken, beef, or pork. Veal Nunzio and Chicken Nunzio are featured on my menu."

INGREDIENTS

8 oz. portion of sliced veal tenderloin
4 oz. white wine
3/4 stick butter
4 oz. crabmeat
2 oz. sliced provel cheese
1/2 fresh squeezed lemon
fresh grilled vegetables (for garnish)
salt and pepper to taste

Pound four 2-ounce veal medallions very thin. Flour, then sauté in 1/4 stick butter. Remove the meat and set aside. Deglaze the pan with four ounces of white wine, 1/2 squeezed lemon, and 1/2 stick of cold butter to make sauce. Salt and pepper to taste. Place veal medallions on a plate, overlapping one another to have a shingle appearance. Place on top: four ounces of fresh crabmeat and two ounce of sliced provel cheese. Bake until cheese melts. Add an appropriate portion of sauce to cover, and garnish with asparagus or fresh grilled vegetables.

SERVES 1

Charlie Gitto's | RECIPES

RISOTTO WITH FRESH TOMATO

"This is a wonderful summer dish which is one of my personal favorites. We use homegrown tomatoes from our garden at the restaurant. In Italy on Sundays after mass, my great-grandmother would prepare this dish to accompany the many fantastic entrees she would serve to family and friends."

INGREDIENTS

4 tbsp. olive oil
2 cups finely chopped onions
2 whole garlic cloves finely chopped
2 lbs. fresh tomatoes seeded, skin removed, and coarsely diced
1/2 stick butter
1 1/2 cups arborio rice
1 cup white wine
2 cups chicken stock
1 cup freshly grated parmesan cheese
1/4 cup fresh chopped basil
salt and pepper to taste

Heat olive oil in a pot. Sauté half of onions and half of garlic until they are light in color. Add tomatoes and simmer approximately 15 to 20 minutes. Purée through strainer and set aside. Melt the butter in a separate large pot and add the remaining onions and garlic until onions are translucent. Add rice and stir. Pour the white wine until half of it evaporates. Add the stock gradually, stirring constantly. The rice should be barely covered with liquid. Cook for 15 to 20 minutes, continuing to stir until rice is done. Stir in the purée and season with salt and pepper to taste. The risotto should have a liquid and creamy consistency. Stir in grated parmesan cheese and garnish with basil.

SERVES 6

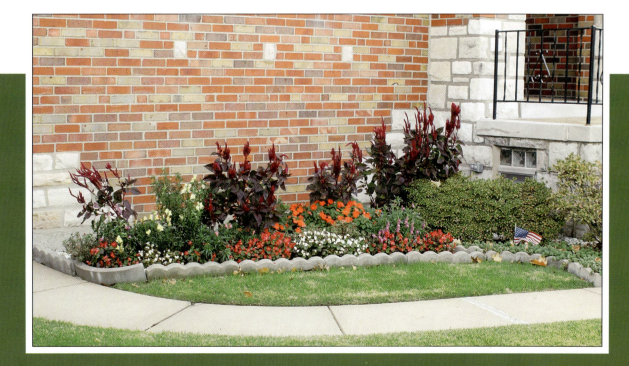

Eggplant Parmigiano

"Eggplant parmigiano is a delicious Gitto recipe. Its tradition stills carries on in my restaurant today. This specialty can be served as an entrée, sidedish, or as an appetizer."

Ingredients

1 medium-sized eggplant, skinned and sliced crossways, 1/2-inch thick
1/2 cup seasoned flour
8 oz. tomato sauce
4 oz. provolone cheese
3 oz. parmesan cheese
4 eggs (beaten)
1 tbsp. fresh parsley

Soak the eggplant in salted water, then remove eggplant after one hour and dry. Dip in egg wash, then in seasoned flour, and fry until golden brown. Pat dry and shingle eggplant on plate. Add tomato sauce, parmesan cheese, and provolone cheese. Bake at 350 degrees until cheese is melted. Sprinkle parsley over the dish.

Serves 2

BONE-IN FILLET

"This is one of the signature dishes at Charlie Gitto's "On the Hill." We were pleased to be the first to introduce this recipe to the St. Louis market. Normally, the bone is taken out of a fillet. Having the bone in allows the juices to be retained, giving the meat a sweeter, more succulent taste. Our bone-in fillet is very popular with our customers."

INGREDIENTS

16 oz. bone-in fillet
1 zucchini
1 squash
1 leek
1 bay leaf
3 tomatoes, with skin on
1 cup sugar
1 cup red wine vinegar
2 tbsp. raisins
1/4 tsp. crushed red pepper
2 cups port wine
1 shallot
2 1/2 cups demi (brown sauce,
     beef broth, or bouillon cubes)
2 oz. meat trimmings
2 oz. butter
salt and pepper to taste
1 oz. balsamic vinegar

Season steak with salt and pepper. Grill to perfection. Wash, cut, and steam vegetables. For chutney: peel, seed, and chop tomatoes. Reduce the vinegar, sugar, bay leaf, and red pepper flakes to a syrupy consistency. Add raisins and chopped tomatoes. Cook until the moisture evaporates. For sauce, brown meat trimmings and shallot. Degrease. Add port wine, simmer, reduce by half. Add demi and reduce by half. Stir in butter and seasonings. Strain and finish with balsamic vinegar.

On a plate with steamed vegetables, tomato and raisin chutney, ladle the sauce over the fillet. Accompany with mashed potatoes.

SERVES 1

Charlie Gitto's | RECIPES

Fresh Stuffed Tilapia

"This is a magnificent dish that everyone can enjoy. It is best served with grilled vegetables or risotto."

Ingredients
1 1/2 lbs. of fresh tilapia, cut in four-inch pieces
salt and pepper to taste

Stuffing:
3 tsp. salted capers
1 garlic clove, finely chopped
4 oz. prosciutto, finely diced
3 tbsp. chopped parsley
1 whole green tomato, diced
1/2 cup seasoned bread crumbs
salt and pepper to taste
1 1/2 tbsp. butter, room temperature

Sauce:
1 1/2 cups fish stock (homemade or store-bought fish base)
3 tbsp. heavy cream
1/2 tsp. thyme
1/2 tsp. basil
white wine to taste
salt and pepper to taste

Season fish with salt and pepper and slice in the middle leaving an inch from the top and bottom. To make the stuffing, first rinse capers in a strainer for about 15 minutes, then dice. In a large mixing bowl, combine the capers, garlic, prosciutto, tomato, parsley, and bread crumbs. Slowly add butter and season with salt and pepper to taste. Place stuffing into the fish; allow a little overflow on top of the fish. Heat oven to 375 degrees and place in oven until it is done. For the sauce, pour the fish stock into a skillet and reduce by half. Strain and place back on burner. Stir in cream and reduce again slightly. Add thyme, basil, white wine, salt, and pepper to taste. Ladle over tilapia.

Serves 4

Chocolate Caramel Cheesecake

A very popular dessert served at Charlie Gitto's "On the Hill." "My son, Anthony Gitto, and I invented this dish for my wife on her 35th birthday." "Mom loves chocolate, caramel and cheesecake. Why not put it all in one?" said Anthony.

Ingredients

- 1 1/2 cups all-purpose flour
- 1/8 tsp. salt
- 1 cup sugar, divided
- 6 tbsp. unsalted butter
- 2 tbsp. vegetable shortening
- 2 to 3 tbsp. ice water
- 1 lb. semi-sweet chocolate, melted
- 2 large packages (8 oz. each) cream cheese, at room temperature
- 3 eggs
- 1 cup caramel
- 1/4 pound pecans

In a large bowl, combine flour, salt and 1/2 cup sugar. Cut in the butter and shortening until the mixture is of a coarse consistency. Add two tablespoons of the ice water and toss to moisten flour. Shape dough into a ball. If any flour does not stick, sprinkle the remaining ice water onto dough. Flatten into a seven-inch disk, wrap tightly and refrigerate for at least four hours or overnight.

Roll out the pastry to a thin round 16-inch diameter. Place it in a 12-inch pan, fitting the dough inside against the sides and trimming any excess off the edges. Refrigerate the pan for 20-25 minutes. Preheat the oven to 350 degrees. Cover with parchment paper and fill with beans to weight paper down. Bake pan in the center of the oven for 25-30 minutes, or until golden brown around the edges. Remove weights and cook an additional five minutes. Beat melted chocolate and cream cheese, adding remaining sugar until light and fluffy. Slowly add eggs one at a time and blend. Fill the warm pie shell with chocolate and cheese mixture. Sprinkle the pecans over the top. Bake pie in the oven. Set timer for 25 minutes, or until set. Let cool to room temperature. Drizzle caramel over the top, slice, and serve.

Serves 8

Charlie Gitto's Lobster Spedini

"Back in the early 1970s, in one of St. Louis' famous restaurants, Rich & Charlie's Trattoria, this recipe was born. Many patrons would travel from all around to enjoy this wonderful dish. We occasionally serve this recipe upon request because of its popularity."

Ingredients

8 oz South African lobster tail cut in one-inch chunks
1 stick butter
1 cup seasoned bread crumbs

Lemon Butter Sauce

1/2 cup clarified butter
1 whole lemon, squeezed
1 tbsp. freshly chopped parsley
1 tsp. freshly chopped garlic

Place lobster on a skewer. Dredge in clarified butter then in seasoned bread crumbs. Mold the lobster around the skewer. Place spedini on open flame and baste with lemon butter sauce until cooked, leaving grill marks. Serve with Risotto Milanese. Spoon over remaining sauce.

Serves 1

Charlie Gitto's | RECIPES

Tenderloin Stuffed with Lobster

"This mouthwatering dish was created by a cousin, the late Charles "Mungo" Mugavero. It has always been a personal favorite of mine. I can recall this colorful character as if he was still here today."

Ingredients

8 oz. center cut prime beef tenderloin
4 oz. South African lobster tail
4 oz lemon sauce
3 oz. prosciutto, diced
1/2 cup fresh button mushrooms
1/2 cup flour
3 oz. olive oil

Lightly dip the lobster in seasoned flour and put aside. Season the fillet with salt and pepper and char grill over an open flame. Remove meat from flame and, using your finger, poke a hole in the center of the fillet and stuff in the lobster. Add in a skillet: lemon sauce, prosciutto, and mushrooms. Cook until mushrooms are tender. Cut the fillet in half exposing the center where lobster is. Pour sauce over the top and garnish with fresh vegetables.

Serves 1

Fresh Tomato and Zucchini Bruschetta

"Bruschetta is a superb Italian appetizer. My mother would have tomato and zucchini bruschetta ready for us when we came home from school. I can still smell the fresh bread baking in the oven. My mother took pride in her fresh homegrown vegetables. From her garden to our kitchen, we enjoyed red, ripe, juicy tomatoes; beautiful, fresh mint; green basil; and richly green zucchini."

Ingredients

1 bunch fresh basil
1 1/2 lbs. tomatoes, peeled, seeded, and diced
1/2 lb. fresh zucchini diced
2 garlic cloves, finely chopped
4 tsp. extra-virgin olive oil
12 slices white Italian bread
salt and pepper to taste

Cut fresh basil into strips, leaving a few whole leaves for a garnish. Combine the basil strips with tomatoes, zucchini, garlic, and oil. Season to taste. Preheat the oven to 450 degrees and toast the slices of fresh Italian bread, or garlic bread, and keep in the oven until lightly toasted on both sides. Remove from the oven, and spoon the tomato mixture on top of the bread. Garnish with whole fresh basil leaves and parmesan cheese.

Serves 6

VEAL CHOP MILANESE STYLE

"This dish was created in the early 1980s when I was in Milan, Italy. I had the pleasure to cook with Chef Salvatore at his restaurant, "Il Latini" in Milan. This dish is also referred to by locals in Italy as "orecchiette all' elefante" (little ear of the elephant). This treasured and magnificent recipe contains the following:"

INGREDIENTS

4 center cut 9 oz. veal chops
4 eggs, beaten
2 cups of seasoned bread crumbs
1 cup flour
1 bunch arugula, sautéed in olive oil and garlic

Take the 9-ounce veal chops and pound until thin, about an 1/8 of an inch thick. Dredge in flour, then dip in egg wash to completely coat the chop. Lastly, place in seasoned bread crumbs. Be sure to totally coat the entire chop in the bread crumbs. Pan sauté in olive oil until golden brown. Garnish with arugula at the top of the bone.

SERVES 4

Note: A photo of this dish appears on the dust jacket.

PENNE BORGHESE

"This is a timeless dish which we serve at Charlie Gitto's 'On the Hill.' This dish was created by Charlie, Jr. along with Ernest Borghese."

INGREDIENTS

6 tbsp. olive oil
1/2 cup finely diced yellow onion
1/2 cup diced prosciutto
3 tbsp. chopped fresh parsley
6 tbsp. cognac
6 oz. tomato sauce
3 cups heavy cream
salt and pepper to taste
1 lb. penne noodles, cooked according to directions on package

Heat oil in a medium sauté pan. Add onion, prosciutto, and parsley and cook until onions are translucent. Remove pan from heat. Drain and remove onion mixture from pan, then set aside. Pour out remaining oil. Pour cognac into pan. Scrape with a wooden spoon to loosen any brown bits. Return onion mixture to pan and return to heat. Add tomato sauce and cream, with salt and pepper to taste. Bring to a simmer and add penne. Cook until penne is hot and sauce has reduced slightly. Serve immediately.

SERVES 4

Dominic's

It is only appropriate that a devoted family man like Dominic Galati should have established his restaurant across from the Hill's St. Ambrose Catholic Church. Somewhat shy and self-effacing, the restauranteur hides behind a welcoming smile and Old World charm. Also fitting is the nearby statue of an immigrant family. Coming from Palermo, Sicily in the late 1960s, Dominic, one of 12 siblings, emigrated at the request of a St. Louis uncle who had tragically lost two sons. In Sicily, after only five years of schooling, Dominic had taken up carpentry. "In my village of Giardinello," he remarks, "where everyone is poor, two carpenters was one carpenter too many."

Not knowing any English, Dominic was first employed making pizzas at Ponticello's on Natural Bridge. As a waiter at Tony's, he fell in love with the barber's daughter, Jackie Ferrante. "Oh those beautiful eyes," he reminisces.

In 1971, the couple sold their newly purchased home to start Dominic's in a two-story, post-World-War-II building. The family, with babies Gina and Maria, lived upstairs while downstairs, Jackie and Dominic invested their life savings, energy, and ambition into the fledgling enterprise. The family apartment is now converted into a banquet room for 50, having put Dominic's early carpentry skills to good use. In this room, Jane Saunder's murals are featured of Palermo, Monte Pellegrino, Positano, and Rome's exquisite Villa Borghese.

Gracious and chivalrous, Dominic greets

Dominic's | RECIPES

and seats his customers. A visible presence, he is well-liked and admired not only by customers but also by his staff. "No matter how menial the task," they affirm, "he pitches in. Dominic treats us like family; he is the best of bosses."

The 160-seat restaurant decorated in Florentine fashion boasts an impressive collection of original oil paintings. These four rooms have seen its share of celebrities—Dean Martin, Sammy Davis, Jr, Liza Minnelli, Tony Bennett, Gene Kelly, Yul Brynner, Rock Hudson, and Michael Keaton. One night, the Galatis hosted Stan Musial, Tony LaRussa, Red Schoendienst, and Joe Torre. "All in one night," muses the restauranteur, "the thrill of a lifetime."

When asked what is the secret of the Hill's success, Dominic affirms "It is the close-knit community and the strong leadership of the parish priest." What is the secret of the Galati's success? A good reputation, longevity, a loyal and savvy staff? It is the personality of Dominic; accommodating, easy going yet fastidious. Devoted to family and the labor of his hands, in spite of his success, he is kept humble by remembering his roots.

The St Ambrose bell tower chimes at six. It announces to friends that it is time to enjoy "the fine dining experience" that has made Dominic's a Hill tradition for many years past and many more to come.

Zuppa di Pesce

A great Italian classic, zuppa di pesce (fish soup), is often a robust stew that constitutes the main course of a meal. The flavorsome soup is traditionally served in deep plates, and poured over a slice of grilled country bread. Almost every major town along the Italian coast varies the recipe. However, what they have in common is the use of a bony but ordinary fish as a source of the flavor, which is then upgraded by the addition of shellfish. Tonno and tonnetto (large and small tuna, respectively) are commonly used as a flavor base. Commercial tuna fisheries in the Mediterranean date back to the early Greeks. In Sicily, the flashing blue tuna are still trapped in long nets, extending out to sea, and then gaffed. This ancient ritual, called the mattanza, was described by Aeschylus (Greek playwright) and continues to be a popular spectacle in May or June along the Sicilian coast.

As for Dominic, he created this soup in memory of his mother. "I remember when the local fisherman would stop by on the corner and the women would come onto the street and examine the assortment of 'fruits of the sea' in his cart. All 12 of us, our mouths would start watering and counting down the minutes until we could dig into this soup with my mother's incredible bread dipped in garlic and olive oil. Lock the doors. We thought we were enjoying a piece of heaven."

Ingredients

3 oz. virgin olive oil
1 small onion
6 cloves of fresh garlic, sliced thin
2 whole tomatoes, peeled, and chopped
1/2 cup dry white wine
1 pinch of red pepper
   if you have favorite spices add them
salt to taste
3 tbsp. chopped fresh parsley
2 cups water
1 loaf Italian bread or any type of firm bread, toasted
12 fresh clams
12 fresh mussels
12 peeled shrimp
12 sea scallops
1 lb. of grouper, red snapper, or any type of meaty fish
   cut into chunks

In a large pan, sauté onion and garlic in olive oil until golden. Add chopped tomatoes, cook for 5 minutes, then add white wine and cook for another 5 minutes. Add the rest of the ingredients and simmer for 10-12 minutes or until cooked. Season to taste. Serve in a bowl with bread on the side. Serve with white wine to complement this dish.

Serves 6

Dominic's | RECIPES

OSSOBUCO (BRAISED VEAL MARROWBONE)

Veal is known for its delicate flavor, less pronounced than a red meat and adapting well to a great variety of combinations. Veal is eaten mainly in Piedmont, Lombardy, and the Veneto, all northern provinces. In Piedmont, the animals are often raised only on cow's milk for twelve months without weaning, and their diet is enriched with egg yolks added to the mother's milk. Although an animal fed this way (sanato) grows to a good size, its flesh retains a delicate flavor sought after by gourmets.

Regarding the following Lombardy-style dish, Dominic affirms, "the secret is in the slow baking so the meat just falls off the bone." A late addition to the menu, Dominic acquiesced to customers who had begged him to add ossobuco. "On a cold winter's day with a red chianti," he comments, "there is nothing more robust and satisfying."

INGREDIENTS

meaty part of a foreleg shinbone of young veal
2 tbsp. butter
1 grated carrot
1/4 cup chopped celery
1 medium onion
pinch of rosemary and sage
2 tbsp. tomato paste
1 cup dry white wine
1/2 cup water or stock
grated rind of small lemon
2 tbsp. finely chopped parsley
1 chopped garlic clove

Halve the meaty part of a foreleg shinbone of young veal sawn into six three-inch pieces. With its surrounding layer of meat, each piece will form an individual circular steak with marrowbone in the center. Brown the pieces on all sides in a heavy pot with two tablespoons butter. Turn the pieces upright with the bones vertical, to hold in the marrow. Add salt and pepper, one small grated carrot, 1/4 cup chopped celery, one medium-sized onion (chopped) with a pinch of rosemary and sage. Cover the pot and simmer for about ten minutes. Blend two tablespoons tomato paste with one cup dry white wine and stir this mixture into the juices. Add 1/2 cup water or stock, cover and simmer over low heat, adding small amounts of liquid from time to time should this be necessary. In about two hours or when the meat is tender, sprinkle in a mixture known as gremolada, made as follows: Combine the grated rind of a small lemon, two tablespoons finely chopped parsley, and one chopped clove of garlic.

Serve with boiled rice or risotto.

SERVES 6

Dominic's | RECIPES

Roast Lamb alla Romana

Olive oil, herbs, such as garlic and rosemary, were in common use at the time of the Roman Empire, hence the "Romana" tag to this classic dish. Dominic remembers in his younger days, sheep and goats grazing on the hillside of his native Sicily. "One was always butchered and served for Easter dinner along with my mother's wonderful homemade St. Joseph's pasta. Twelve children at the table and no one dared move or breathe, we were so excited about enjoying this feast." For many years, Dominic has done a featured recipe, including this one, on Channel 5 Show Me St. Louis. His philosophy in cooking is "Keep it simple." Involved, complicated dishes have no place in his kitchen. "That way cooking becomes something to look forward to, and not a chore." The following roast lamb is an example of simple yet classic cooking.

Ingredients

1/2 leg of lamb (about three lbs.)
3 garlic cloves cut into thin slivers
1 oz. of olive oil
1 tbsp. of fresh rosemary
1 small onion coarsely chopped
salt and freshly ground black pepper
1/2 cup vegetable stock
1 1/2 lbs. of potatoes cut into quarters
1 lb. of cooked baby carrots

Preheat the oven to 450 degrees. Using the point of a sharp knife, make a deep incision into the lamb and insert the slivers of garlic. Put the lamb in a roasting pan and rub it all over with half of the olive oil. Sprinkle on about half of the rosemary. Season with salt and a grinding of pepper. Roast for 30 minutes, turning once. Lower the oven heat to 375 degrees. Add the red wine, the onions, and the vegetable stock. Roast for an hour and fifteen minutes to an hour and a half, or until the lamb is tender. During the roasting, turn the lamb, basting each time it is turned.

Meanwhile, put the potatoes in a separate roasting pan and toss with the remaining olive oil and rosemary. Salt and pepper to taste. Roast for 45 minutes, turning the potatoes several times until they are golden and tender. Transfer the lamb to a carving board tent with foil, and set aside in a warm place for five minutes.

Carve the lamb into thin slices, and place them on a large serving platter alongside the roasted potatoes and cooked carrots. Strain the juice. Pour over the lamb and serve.

Serves 4

Dominic's | RECIPES

PETTI DI VITELLO RIPIENO (Stuffed Veal Breast)

The following is a rich Piedmontese dish belonging to the tradition of Turin, which means it was created in the kitchens of the Royal Palace or of an aristocratic family in the eighteenth century when the fashion, including that of food, was dictated by the splendor of the French Court of Versailles. Dominic's romantic restaurant with its elegant atmosphere has been the scene of many a special celebration. One of the most popular dinner choices for such an occasion, according to Kim, his tuxedoed waitress, is the following veal dish. Kim, who has worked for Dominic for twelve years, relates "I like the food here so much that when my husband proposed to me, Dominic's is the place I chose for my engagement dinner!"

INGREDIENTS

1/2 lb. spinach trimmed
1/2 cup grated parmigiano cheese
2 eggs
1 lb. breast of veal
2 oz. thinly sliced prosciutto ham
1 clove fresh garlic chopped
2 tbsp. butter
2 tbsp. olive oil
2 sprigs of sage
2 rosemary sprigs
1/2 cup dry white wine
1/2 cup beef stock
1/2 cup flour

Preheat oven to 350 degrees. Boil spinach in a small amount of salted water. Drain spinach completely and set aside to cool. After cooled, place in a bowl and mix along with parmigiano cheese, eggs and garlic, adding salt and pepper to taste. Pound veal with mallet until flattened (1/4 inch thick). Lightly salt veal and spread spinach mixture on entire breast, finishing with slices of prosciutto ham. Roll up veal, closing it well around the filling and tie tightly with a string. In a skillet, gently warm oil and butter, adding sage and rosemary. Sauté over moderate heat. Lightly flour the veal and brown all sides while adding wine, salt, and beef stock. Sauté about ten minutes. Place in a covered pan and cook for 35 minutes, turning each piece every 10 minutes. To ensure moist veal, you may add 1/2 tablespoon stock. Remove the lid and increase temperature to 400 degrees, cooking for another ten minutes. Remove string, slice, and serve.

SERVES 4   *Note: A photo of this dish appears on page 1 of this book.*

Fettuccine alla Bolognese

Fettuccine bolognese features a regional meat sauce made famous in Bologna–an Italian city between Florence and Rome. In northern Italy, butter and cheese are the most popular ingredients for serving with pasta. Children, in particular, love this dish. This is a very happy mating of one of the great sauces with the prince of all noodles. Very few ingredients are needed to make up such an incredibly simple dish. As the sauce is so rich, less butter and cheese are needed, but the procedure is the same. Serve in hot bowls, with the piping hot sauce lavishly topping each serving.

Since 1971, fettuccine bolognese has proved a popular Dominic's staple. This signature item helps Dominic's maintain its Travel and Holiday *magazine dining awards and Mobil 4-star accreditation.*

Ingredients

3 tbsp. olive oil
1 small onion, finely chopped
1 carrot, finely chopped
1 celery stick, finely chopped
2 garlic cloves, crushed
12 oz. ground beef
2/3 cup red wine
1 cup water
1 cup milk
1 can (14 oz.) chopped tomatoes
1 tbsp. tomato paste
12 oz. dried fettuccine
1 pinch grated nutmeg
1 tbsp. shredded fresh basil
1 bay leaf
salt and freshly ground black pepper
parmigiano cheese

Heat the oil in a large saucepan. Add the onion, carrot, celery, and garlic; cook gently. Stir frequently for 10 minutes or until softened. Add the ground beef to the pan with the vegetables and cook over medium heat until the meat changes color. Stirring constantly, break up any lumps with a wooden spoon. Pour in wine and stir frequently. When the liquid has evaporated, add the milk and continue cooking and stirring until this, too, has evaporated. Stir in the tomatoes, tomato paste, nutmeg, bay leaf, and half the basil with salt and pepper to taste. Simmer the sauce uncovered, over the lowest possible heat for at least one hour. Cook the fettuccine in a large pan of rapidly boiling, salted water for eight to ten minutes or until al dente. Drain thoroughly and pour into a warm bowl. Pour on the sauce and toss to combine. Garnish with the rest of the basil and serve immediately with parmigiano cheese.

Serves 4

Dominic's | RECIPES

RECIPES | Dominic's

Zuppa per le Feste (Holiday Soup)

Meatballs *(omit for vegetarian version)*
7 oz. of lean ground hamburger
1 whole egg
1/4 cup of bread crumbs
1/4 cup parmigiano cheese
salt and pepper

Ingredients
3 tbsp. olive oil
1 small carrot chopped
1 small onion chopped
1 tomato peeled and diced
2 cloves of fresh garlic finely chopped
2 oz. of fresh spinach chopped
7 cups of beef or chicken broth
3 tbsp. fresh parsley chopped
2 cups of cooked rice
1/4 cup grated parmigiano cheese
salt and pepper

Mix together meatball ingredients and make very small meatballs. Preheat the oven to 400 degrees, and bake for 5 minutes. Set aside.

In medium saucepan, heat the oil, stir in the onion, and cook for five minutes. Add the carrots, tomato, garlic, and spinach. Cook over moderate heat, stirring often for five minutes.

Pour in the hot broth and stir well, add salt and pepper. Bring to a boil. Add the meatballs, and simmer in moderate heat for two minutes. Stir in the rice and sprinkle in the parsley. Allow the soup to stand for a few minutes then serve with grated parmigiano cheese.

Serves 6

If you want to cook Italian, and you want to cook Italian well, the Hill has many Italian food markets such as Volpi's, Viviano's, Urzi's, and DiGregorio's. Shown are Dorothy, John, and Toni at DiGregorio's Market.

Dominic's | # RECIPES

GIARDINELLO GRILLED EGGPLANT (SUMMER APPETIZER)

The eggplant is first cousin to the tomato. It reached Sicily during the Middle Ages from the East, but Sicilians never ate the vegetable, fearing it to be poisonous. The story goes that during a famine, the Sicilians first tested eggplant on their goats, who ate them and survived. In the sixteenth century, in fact, the Italian word for eggplant, melanzana, was thought to derive from the Latin "malum insanum," meaning "unhealthy sickness."

Giardinello is a tiny village near Palermo, Sicily where Dominic and his eleven brothers and sisters were raised. His godfather helped him come to St. Louis, where the young emigrant carried the memory of his family in his heart and his mother's recipes in his head. The following is one of the latter.

INGREDIENTS
1 whole eggplant
2 fresh tomatoes peeled and chopped
1/4 cup chopped onions
2 cloves of chopped fresh garlic
1/2 cup olive oil
10 oz. fresh mozzarella cheese
1/4 cup chopped basil leaves
salt and fresh ground pepper

Cut the eggplant in half-inch thick slices. Season with salt and pepper and brush each side with half of the olive oil. Grill (or broil) on both sides for five minutes. Combine the onions, tomatoes, garlic, and fresh basil. Sauté in a skillet for about five minutes, add the eggplant, and season to taste. Move everything into a baking dish. Spread mozzarella cheese on each slice of the eggplant. Bake at 400 degrees until cheese is melted.

SERVES 4

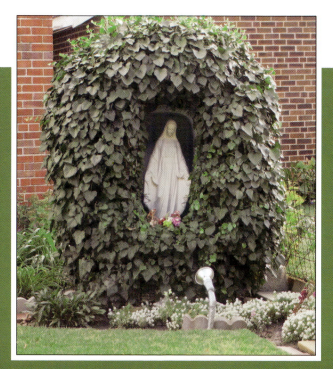

Tiramisu

A unique and enjoyable dessert, "tiramisu" means "pick me up," which is appropriate for this delicious dessert which contains a shot of strong coffee. There are different versions of this tremendously successful dish, but the most common version is included here. It is not known who created the original recipe, but it is believed to have been a cook between Venice and Treviso in the north where tiramisu spread like wildfire before taking over the whole country.

According to Dominic, the version popular in his restaurant is considered a classic style because it uses sweet Marsala wine, an addition he remembers his mother and sisters made. When asked if his family ever wanted to emigrate, he waxes wistful and says, "Unfortunately, no. At one point I had all the papers made out but time passed, and they were committed to their lives in Sicily so they never came." Dominic's favorite dessert is spumoni or vanilla ice cream, or an occasional Ted Drewes vanilla concrete.

Ingredients

1 cup sugar
6 large eggs separated
12 oz. mascarpone cheese
1/4 cup sweet Marsala wine
1 cup espresso coffee
36 ladyfingers
unsweetened cocoa powder
  for dusting
3 oz. semi-sweet chocolate grated
1/2 oz. of Sambuca (liqueur)

In a large bowl or in the bowl of an electric mixer, beat the egg yolks with the sugar and mascarpone until texture is creamy. Add the Sambuca. Then whip the egg whites until soft peaks are formed and fold in with previous mixture.

Combine the espresso and Marsala wine in a bowl and quickly dip the ladyfingers in the mixture. Place one half of them in a single layer in a rectangular glass casserole. Then spread a layer of half the ingredients of paragraph one. Repeat with the remaining ladyfingers. Lay them the opposite direction of the bottom layer and add the remaining cheese and egg mixture. Sprinkle the grated chocolate and dust the entire top of cake with cocoa. Chill for four hours.

Optional: Garnish with seasonal berries before serving.

Serves 8

Dominic's | RECIPES

Farfalle alla Karman

*Dominic named this dish after a longtime family friend who loved it so much, it became her namesake.
"Farfalle means 'butterflies', but they are usually called bow tie pasta in this country."*

Ingredients
- 1 cup wild mushrooms sliced
- 1 oz. of virgin olive oil
- 2 tbsp. butter
- 1 small onion finely chopped
- 1 large tomato peeled and chopped
- 2 garlic cloves crushed
- 1 oz. ham cut into matchsticks
- 2 tbsp. fresh parsley finely chopped
- 2/3 cup dry white wine
- 2/3 cup grated parmesan cheese
- 1/2 cup 40% cream
- 1 lb. dried farfalle noodles
- 1/2 cup frozen peas

In a large pan heat olive oil and sauté the ham, onion, and garlic, stirring for about three minutes, until the onion is soft. Add tomato, mushrooms, and peas. Cook for about five minutes. Add the wine, and simmer for three minutes. Add cream and butter, simmer for five minutes. Then add salt and plenty of black pepper to taste. Cook the farfalle in a large saucepan in rapidly boiling salted water for about ten minutes, or until al dente. Drain the pasta thoroughly, add to the sauce, and toss with cheese and parsley to mix. Taste for seasoning and serve immediately with some extra parmesan cheese on the side.

Serves 4

Petti di Pollo alla Gina

This recipe is a favorite of his oldest daughter, Gina, who studies at the Music Conservatory in Kansas City. The dark-haired and dark-eyed future opera singer is the "spitting image of her mother."

Ingredients
- 4 pieces chicken breast
- 3 tbsp. virgin olive oil
- 1 tbsp. chopped parsley
- 4 tbsp. chicken stock
- 3 oz. of prosciutto ham, diced
- 1/2 cup flour
- 3 tbsp. butter
- 1 oz. dry white wine
- 3 oz. fontina cheese
- 4 tbsp. tomato sauce

Select four pieces of chicken breast, free from all skin and bone. Slice into thin cutlets, and flatten the slices as much as possible. The thinner the slices, the more delicate the dish will become. Dredge chicken with flour. Brown the slices lightly on each side, using three tablespoons of olive oil and three tablespoons of butter heated together in a skillet. Season the slices with salt and pepper. Coat each one with a thin slice of fontina cheese and finely diced prosciutto ham. Add four tablespoons of tomato sauce, four tablespoons of chicken stock, and one ounce dry white wine. Put the pan into a slow oven at 325 degrees, until the cheese has melted and the sauce has slightly thickened. Serve each slice of chicken breast on a hot serving dish with the sauce poured over each slice of chicken. Serve with asparagus, mushrooms, and mashed potatoes on the side. Sprinkle the tablespoon of parsley over the chicken and enjoy.

Serves 4

Spaghetti with Basil and Tomato Pesto alla Jackie

Dominic met Jackie, his wife of 36 years, when he waited tables at Tony's in the 1960s. His eyes get misty remembering, and it is easy to see that this pragmatic restauranteur is a romantic at heart and very dependent on his bride and business partner. At home, on a family Sunday, Dominic grills steak and vegetables and prepares the following pasta dish.

Ingredients
- 1 lb. spaghetti
- 1 cup fresh basil leaves
- 4 cloves of fresh garlic crushed and peeled
- 2 whole fresh tomatoes chopped and peeled
- 1 1/2 cups pecorino cheese
- 8 tbsp. virgin olive oil
- salt and freshly ground black pepper

Place the garlic, basil, olive oil, tomatoes, and one half of the cheese in a blender and process to a thick paste. Cook the spaghetti in lightly salted water for ten minutes or until al dente. Drain well. Spoon the pesto onto the hot pasta and toss lightly until melted. Sprinkle on the rest of the cheese and serve.

Serves 4

Spaghetti with Broccoli and Shrimp alla Maria

According to the wait staff, Dominic and Jackie's youngest daughter, Maria, is a "mini-Dominic" bristling with personality, enthusiasm and ambition. Maria is a second-year student at Lindenwood College. This dish was named after the future restauranteur.

Ingredients
- 12 oz. spaghetti
- 4 tbsp. virgin olive oil
- 1 small onion chopped
- 2 cloves garlic chopped
- 3 large peeled tomatoes chopped
- 12 large shrimp peeled, deveined, and cleaned
- 2 tsp. of chopped parsley
- pinch of crushed red pepper and salt to taste
- 1/2 cup white wine
- 1/2 lb. broccoli florets coarsely cut
- grated cheese of your preference (optional)

Heat the oil in a saucepan. Add the onion and cook gently, stirring for about three minutes. Add garlic, tomato, broccoli, and cook for five minutes. Add shrimp, simmer for five minutes. Add wine and simmer for three minutes. Add parsley, and stir thoroughly. Set aside. Cook the spaghetti in a large saucepan in rapidly boiling water for about ten minutes, or until "al dente." Drain the pasta thoroughly, add the sauce and toss. Add a pinch of crushed red pepper and salt to taste. Serve immediately.

Serves 4

Giovanni's

Ann Lemons Pollack, in an article for *St. Louis Magazine,* has crowned Giovanni "The King of the Hill." The current and previous three presidents; Michael Jordan; Paul McCartney of Beatles' fame; Oprah Winfrey; and many celebrities have graced the private dining rooms of Giovanni's award-winning restaurant. It does not take a visitor long to see that the Gabrieles–Giovanni and Frank, father and son–have a knack for making everyone who visits their restaurant feel like a celebrity.

Immediately upon entering Giovanni's, the host warmly welcomes and greets you in full formal attire. Recessed Greek statues and museum-quality original paintings adorn the interior. Giovanni Gabriele, a natural-born promoter, introduces himself and relates the journey that brought him to St. Louis thirty-nine years ago from Palermo, Sicily. After arriving, he then sought out and married his childhood sweetheart, Serafina. He worked as a combustion engineer by day and a restauranteur by night. "I fell in love with America and I have a beautiful wife at my side," says Giovanni in his charming, broken English. "When we opened our restaurant in 1973 with only my two sons, Carmelo and Frank, I put napkins over their little arms to serve the food. That was only the beginning. The two children grew up and continued to work in the food industry. They are now recognized as two of the finest young chefs in the country. Cooking is in an Italian's blood. If you do not have imagination, you cannot be a good chef."

"In 1980," he continues, "a miracle happened. I received an envelope from President Reagan and the White House. I still keep it to this day. His Inaugural Committee selected one restaurant from each state for Taste of America. I was asked to bring my best recipe and prepare a special dish in Washington during the festivities. After this publicity, my restaurant became a hot spot. President Clinton has eaten here, as well as President George Bush, Sr. Vice President Gore dined with us in 1999 when he was campaigning for the presidency. Of course, Congressman Gephardt is a regular. I liked George W. Bush when he visited. He likes chicken, so I named Involtini di Pollo al Presidente Bush in his honor. He's a good-looking man; he makes you feel very comfortable. Clinton was the same way. However, President Reagan was my favorite and he gave me a big hug.

"When Oprah came, my wife was so excited. Oprah is a sweet lady. I said to her, 'Mrs. Oprah, I'll make a special dish for you. If you like it, I'll name it for you–Pappardelle alla Bella Oprah.' Oprah exclaimed, 'Everybody, come celebrate! I've never had a dish named after me!' I love this lady. She called me the very next week and asked me to appear on her show to prepare her special dish."

Frank Gabriele, Giovanni's son and executive chef, comes out of the kitchen wearing a chef's hat and apron. Frank, like his father before him, believes that food is a living, breathing entity. As part of a new breed of restauranteurs, he is combining the best of the old with the taste of the new. As is common on the Hill, the Giovanni dynasty is being passed from father to son.

BRACIOLE DI PESCESPADA

This is a very typical Italian dish. It is most often found in Messina, Sicily, but one may also find it in other parts of Italy, especially in family-owned trattorias. According to Giovanni, in his native Sicily this dish was originally prepared with salami, cheese, and hardboiled eggs. "We modified it to accommodate American tastes."

INGREDIENTS

1/2 lb. small piece of swordfish
1 small onion, finely chopped
1/4 cup olive oil
2 1/2 tbsp. brandy
salt
2 1/2 tbsp. soft bread crumbs
6 thin slices swordfish
6 slices Mozzarella cheese
2-3 sprigs basil, finely chopped
pinch finely chopped thyme
pepper
1-2 lemons

Wash and dry the small slices of swordfish and mix with the onion. Heat the olive oil in a pan and sauté the fish and onion. As soon as the onion begins to brown, add the brandy and sprinkle lightly with salt. When the brandy is evaporated, take the pan from the heat and add bread crumbs.

Wash and wipe the sliced swordfish. Spread each slice with the cooked swordfish, onion and bread crumb mixture. Cover with a slice of Mozzarella and sprinkle with herbs and freshly ground pepper. Roll up the slices to enclose the filling and tie with thread.

Broil or grill the swordfish rolls, over charcoal if possible, for about 15 minutes. The heat should not be too fierce. Serve immediately, garnish with lemon quarters.

SERVES 6

Giovanni's | RECIPES

RECIPES | *Giovanni's*

Veal Saltimbocca alla Giovanni's

"What makes veal saltimbocca a traditional dish," announces Giovanni, "is the prosciutto and fresh sage topping off sautéed veal. I also add fontinella cheese and this combination of cheese, prosciutto, fresh sage, and white wine makes all the difference." Elaborating upon a critical point of his business philosophy, Giovanni explains, "Never cheat on food quality. We maintain customer loyalty not only because of our classic combination of ingredients, but also because of our impeccable quality. The customer spends big money, so we must also."

Ingredients
12 small veal scallopini
12 slices Volpi Italian ham
12 sage leaves
6 tbsp. butter
salt and pepper
1/2 cup dry white wine
3 tbsp. veal or beef stock
1/2 cup grated fontinella cheese

Carefully beat the scallopini with a cutlet bat until very thin. On each piece place a slice of ham and a sage leaf. Secure with a short toothpick. Do not roll up.

Melt the butter in a wide pan, add the veal slices and brown them on both sides over a brisk heat for a few minutes. Salt lightly, remembering the ham is already salty. Sprinkle with pepper. Add the wine and the stock. The cooking time should be no more than five minutes in all. Sprinkle the fontinella cheese on top and let melt for a minute or two. Serve very hot, arranged on a serving dish, with the sauce spooned over the veal.

Serves 6

Giovanni's | RECIPES

RECIPES | *Giovanni's*

ZUCCHINI RIPIENI DI CARNE

"In Italy in the summer," comments Giovanni, *"the outside markets are so beautiful. They have three different kinds of eggplant, red and yellow peppers, very tender asparagus, sweet peas, and even orange zucchini blossoms. In this dish, only the regular green zucchini is used. This recipe is my son Frank's creation. We use this one like a side dish or an appetizer."*

INGREDIENTS
12 zucchini (large)
2 tbsp. butter
2 1/2 tbsp. olive oil
2 tbsp. ham fat, finely chopped
1 small onion, finely chopped
4 tbsp. tomato paste
salt and pepper
2-3 sprigs parsley, finely chopped

STUFFING
1 1/4 cups ground lean beef
2 eggs
4 tbsp. grated parmesan cheese
2-3 tbsp. fresh bread crumbs
2 oz. ham, finely chopped
salt and pepper
milk – optional

Wash zucchini, cut off the stem end and scoop out the pulp through the stem end with an apple corer, taking care not to break the shell.

Mix together the stuffing ingredients; if the mixture seems a little too thick, add enough milk to loosen it. Stuff the mixture into the zucchini, pushing it in firmly. Heat the butter and oil in a large, wide frying pan, and sauté the ham fat and onion over a low heat until the onion begins to change color. Add the stuffed zucchini and sauté gently, turning them over from time to time to brown evenly but lightly. Dilute the tomato paste with a cup of warm water and pour over the zucchini. Check seasoning, add the parsley, cover and cook gently until tender, about ten minutes. Handle the zucchini carefully when removing from pan or they will break.

SERVES 4-6

Giovanni's | RECIPES

Vitello con Melanzane

"My family and I travel to Italy quite a bit," remarks Giovanni, "and this is a dish we brought back some time ago. I believe that lightly sautéed veal and eggplant with fresh tomato makes for a beautiful combination."

Ingredients

6 thin slices veal fillet
2 large eggplants
salt
olive oil
5 large ripe tomatoes
*1/2 cup green or black
    olives, pitted*
3-4 leaves basil, finely chopped
3 tbsp. butter
flour
6 tbsp. grated parmigiano cheese
6 fresh basil leaves

Wipe eggplants with damp cloth, peel and slice them thinly. Sprinkle with salt and leave in a colander or on a tilted plate to drain away their bitter juices. Wipe dry. Heat plenty of oil in a deep frying pan and fry the eggplants, a few slices at a time, until golden brown on both sides. Take from the pan with a perforated spoon and drain on paper towels. Put aside.

Drain off all but four tablespoons of oil from the pan. Peel and chop the tomatoes, discarding seeds, and cook them in the oil for 10 minutes over high heat. Add salt to taste, the olives, chopped basil, and the eggplant. Lower heat and simmer for 5 minutes. Melt butter in a frying pan. Dust the veal slices with flour and fry quickly for two minutes on each side until browned (add more butter if needed). Take the veal slices from the pan and place them in one layer in a shallow earthenware baking dish. Add a few tablespoons of the tomato sauce, then layer the eggplant on top, and pour on the remaining sauce. Sprinkle parmigiano cheese and top off with the fresh basil leaves. Bake in a moderate oven at 375 degrees for three or four minutes. Serve hot.

Serves 6

Melanzana alla Conca d'Oro

"Paul McCartney came here in 1997 with his wife, Linda," remembers Giovanni. "She was a very sweet lady. Early in the evening, his bodyguard came in and announced that the McCartney party of ten wanted a room to themselves, with nobody seated at any surrounding tables. After the group arrived, Mr. McCartney caused such a sensation among the guests, I called my daughter and asked, 'Who is Paul McCartney?' My daughter laughed and said, 'The Beatles, Dad.' Now Frank Sinatra, I knew who he was when he came in. But McCartney, I did'nt recognize the name. At his request, we prepared six special vegetarian dishes. That was a challenge. The one he liked the most was melanzana alla conca d'oro. That's the only time Paul McCartney spoke to me and to my son, Frank." According to Chef Frank, "When I came out of the kitchen, McCartney seemed very nice. He said 'Chef, you've been so kind and done so much for me and for my family. Is there anything I can do for you?' I asked to have a photo taken with him. Evidently, he does not allow his photo to be taken with anyone–so he just sat down again. We found Oprah to be much more open. She allowed us to have our pictures taken with her. In fact, anyone in the room was welcome to pose with her." Note: conca d'oro means "crown of gold" and is the symbol for Sicily, where this dish originated.

Ingredients

1 large eggplant
1/2 tsp. fresh garlic chopped
2 ripened tomatoes
1/4 lb. fresh basil
1 oz. yellow onion diced
1 serving spoon extra virgin olive oil
2 oz. romano cheese
6 oz. anelletti noodles

Garnish

1/4 lb. fresh basil
1 garlic clove
1 tbsp. extra virgin olive oil
(Place all garnish ingredients in food processor for one minute.)

Halve eggplant and level bottom and top to stand erect. Hollow out middle of eggplant to one inch from skin. Do not go beyond one inch or eggplant will collapse. Marinate eggplant with olive oil and season with salt and pepper. Place eggplant in broiler, rotating from side to side every 1-2 minutes. Total cooking time is 8-10 minutes. Remove eggplant and let it cool.

Take meat from center of eggplant and chop finely. Pour olive oil into skillet, set over medium heat, add garlic and yellow onion and sauté until caramelized. Add eggplant meat and tomatoes. Cook together until eggplant browns, stirring continuously. Once cooked, add basil with salt and pepper to taste.

Cook pasta in a pot of lightly salted water until al dente. When cooked, drain pasta. **NOTE** Some brands of anelletti pasta such as Del Verde or De Cecco take 12 to 15 minutes to cook.

Add pasta to sauce and warm in skillet for one minute, then stuff into eggplant. Top with romano cheese and bake in oven at 350 degrees, for 3-5 minutes. Prepare garnish and serve.

Serves 2

Giovanni's | RECIPES

159

RECIPES | *Giovanni's*

Farfalline del Presidente Reagan

Giovanni prepared this dish for President Reagan's Inaugural Celebration in Washington D.C. in 1980. "I was contacted by Reagan's Inaugural Committee responsible for Taste of America," he reminisces. "They told me, 'We will pay for your transportation and your food costs. We ask only that you bring your special recipe. I called upon Ravarino & Freschi, the St. Louis based pasta company, and asked them to develop a pasta that would remain firm, without becoming mushy. It was important that the pasta hold up for five hours so as to feed ten thousand people every day. We selected farfalline noodles made from a blend of semolina and other types of flour. I shipped seven hundred pounds to feed forty thousand people in four days. I was stationed in the basement of the Treasury Building where there were gigantic stoves. The pots were as big as tables and you used a foot elevator to move the tubs of boiling water up and down. I didn't sleep the entire four days. It was also exciting to have St. Louis' Karen Foss and many other television news personalities interview me."

Ingredients

1 lb. farfalline (bow tie pasta)
salt and pepper to taste
4 oz. butter (unsalted)
4 oz. smoked salmon (cut into cubed pieces)
1 cup grated parmigiano cheese
1 cup cream (40%)

Bring a large pan of salted water to a rapid boil and add the farfalline. Cook al dente five to seven minutes then drain, leaving the farfalline in the hot pan. Add the butter and salmon and let cook for two minutes. Add the cream, cook at a low heat until the cream and butter are married (amalgamated) together. Make sure you have a good cream sauce with farfalline. At this point, sprinkle with salt and fresh pepper to taste, add the parmigiano cheese and toss once or twice. Serve hot immediately.

SERVES 4

LA RIBOLLITA

"I brought this dish back from Genoa. We were on a cruise on a very beautiful Italian ship, the Costa Romantica *for seven days to seven cities. This dish is basically meat cooked for a long time with a lot of vegetables. I changed their recipe from red onions to leeks because I know my customers like it better this way." Giovanni's minestrone is usually made in a large quantity so the next day, there will be enough left over to make ribollita, literally meaning "reboiled." Most Italians prefer ribollita, instead of the minestrone itself, as a popular standard winter dish which is often found on most trattoria menus.*

INGREDIENTS

12 1/2 cups dried white beans soaked overnight
2-3 tbsp. olive oil
1 clove garlic, finely chopped
1 onion, finely chopped
1 carrot, finely chopped
1 stalk celery, finely chopped
2 leeks, finely chopped
1 sprig rosemary, finely chopped
small piece hot chili pepper
1 ham bone
salt and pepper

GARNISH

3/4 cup olive oil
2 cloves garlic crushed
pinch thyme
8 slices bread toasted
3/4 cup grated parmesan cheese
1 onion thinly sliced

Drain the beans. Heat the olive oil in a large pan and gently sauté the garlic, onion, carrot, celery, leeks, rosemary, and the piece of chili pepper until they begin to turn brown. Add the beans and ham bone. Cover with water, season with salt and pepper, and simmer very gently for about two hours, or until beans are tender. Remove the ham bone and rub half the beans through a fine sieve (or purée in a blender). Return the purée to the soup.

Heat 3/4 cup olive oil, sauté the crushed garlic clove, and add thyme until golden. Strain half the oil into the soup and discard the garlic. Stir the soup well.

Arrange slices of toast at the bottom of a fireproof tureen, sprinkle with half the parmesan cheese and pour the soup over the top. Cover with onion slices and add the rest of the oil and grated cheese. Cook in moderate oven at 375 degrees for about half an hour.

SERVES 6-8

RECIPES | *Giovanni's*

OSSOBUCO MILANESE

"Ossobuco," states Giovanni, "is a very old dish and very traditional. They made it two ways: Romana or Milanese. The difference between the two is only the grated lemon in the Milanese. In America, it first appeared in New York. For some reason, there are certain things that are very popular on the East Coast and in Italy, then you try to introduce them to St. Louis. But it takes time for them to catch on. Then it becomes popular. Ossobuco is like that. We were the first restaurant that I know of to bring it here, and now it is a signature item on our menu. In Italy, the marrow of the bone is a delicacy."

INGREDIENTS

6 slices shin bone of veal
flour
6 tbsp. butter
1/2 cup dry white wine
14 oz. can Italian tomatoes peeled
salt and pepper
1 clove garlic, finely chopped or minced
grated rind of 1/2 lemon
3-4 sprigs of parsley, finely chopped
1-2 anchovy fillets, finely chopped

Roll the bones in flour. In a large pan, fry the bones in butter, turning them once or twice to ensure even browning. Pour the wine over them and cook for 15 minutes, then add the tomatoes and season to taste with salt and pepper. Cover and cook for two hours over a low heat until the meat is so tender it almost falls off the bone. If necessary, some hot stock or water may be added during cooking.

Prepare a gremolada, an essential addition to the ossobuco. Mix the garlic, lemon rind, parsley, and anchovy together. Sprinkle this over the bones a few minutes before serving, turning them once to distribute the flavor of the gremolada.

Ossobuco is always served with a large dish of rice, usually risotto Milanese. An important part of the dish is the marrow from the bones. Dig out the marrow using a small narrow fork. The marrow may simply be dug out with the point of a knife and spread on small chunks of bread.

SERVES 6

Giovanni's | RECIPES

163

RISOTTO CON LA ZUCCA

"This recipe," remarks Giovanni, "I found in Milano. I brought it here and put it on my menu. Zucca is pumpkin. You peel it, you slice it, and fry it. In Milano, the one I ate was made with spices like oregano. You must make it your own though; so you modify and you adjust. In Italy, there is more of a European flavor for European tastes. This recipe can serve as a main dish or appetizer."

INGREDIENTS
About 2 lbs. pumpkin
6 tbsp. butter
2-1/2 tbsp. olive oil
About 2 cups boiling water
salt
2-1/2 cups arborio rice
3/4 cup grated parmesan cheese

Peel pumpkin and discard the seeds. Cut the flesh into small pieces.

Heat half the butter and all the oil in a large pan. Sauté the onion very gently until soft, but not brown. Add the pumpkin, pour over one cup boiling water, season to taste with salt and continue cooking for ten minutes, or until pumpkin is tender.

Stir rice into pumpkin thoroughly but gently, and continue cooking until it has absorbed the liquid. Pour in another cup of boiling water until all the water has been absorbed and the rice is tender. This will take about 20 minutes.

Stir in the remaining butter and the cheese very gently, cover the pan, and leave the risotto for two minutes to settle. Serve hot, sprinkled generously with additional grated parmesan cheese.

SERVES 6

CREMA AL MASCARPONE

"Sometimes people don't like tiramisu because they don't like either ladyfingers or a strong espresso taste in a dessert. So we offer them crema al mascarpone as another choice here at Giovanni's."

INGREDIENTS
1 lb. fresh mascarpone cheese
1/2 cup granulated sugar
4 egg yolks
4 egg whites
1/2 cup rum
4-6 plain cookies

Mix the cheese and sugar together, and add the egg yolks, one at a time, beating constantly. Add the rum (brandy may be used instead, if preferred). Fold in the egg whites, scoop the mixture into individual glasses, and chill for several hours. Serve with plain cookies. Buon appetito!

SERVES 4-6

Calamaretti delle Marche

"Large calamari or squid," describes Giovanni, "are tough, but the baby ones, calamaretti, are tender. We make this dish two ways: fritte, fried with olive oil, or with spicy tomato sauce. This is the fried one our customers like."

Ingredients

3 lbs. baby squid
salt
1/2 cup olive oil
2 cloves garlic, crushed
3-4 sprigs parsley, finely chopped
small piece hot chili pepper, finely chopped
1 cup dry white wine
2/3 cup hot stock

Clean squid, by rinsing thoroughly in salted water and dry well. Heat oil and fry the garlic until golden brown; discard the garlic and add the squid, parsley, a little salt and the chili pepper. Cook over a brisk heat for about ten minutes. Moisten with the wine and let it heat. Cover and simmer gently for about 15 minutes longer, or until squid are tender.

Serves 6

Spaghettini Aromatici

"Anchovy, mint, parsley, capers — ingredients like this," declares Giovanni, "create an aroma. That is why I call it aromatici. This is so delicious, I like to see my customers when they place my food under their nose, smell the aroma, and smile. This is one of my creations."

Ingredients

1 1/2 lbs. spaghettini (very fine spaghetti)
1 cup olive oil
2 cloves garlic, crushed
3-4 large anchovy fillets chopped
4 leaves mint finely chopped
3 sprigs parsley finely chopped
4 tsp. capers
12 black olives pitted and chopped

Bring a large pan of salted water to a boil and throw in the spaghettini. Cover, bring the water back to the boil and give the noodles a good stir with a fork. Cook briskly until tender but still firm.

Meanwhile, heat the oil in a pan. Add the garlic cloves, sauté until brown and discard them. Then add the anchovies and cook gently, stirring until they are completely dissolved to a paste. Take the pan from the heat and stir in the mint and parsley. Drain the spaghettini, pour into a heated dish and add the anchovy-flavored oil mixture, the capers and the olives. Mix well, serve, in this case without cheese.

The quantity of olive oil may be increased for those who are particularly fond of it.

Serves 6

RECIPES | Cunetto's

Cunetto's

On any given Friday night, it is guaranteed that the longest line on the Hill will be at Cunetto House of Pasta. If there was a People's Choice Award for "Best Restaurant on the Hill," many say Cunetto's would win, hands down. It didn't start off that way.

Over the bar at Cunetto's, is a three-foot square photograph of two pharmacists with Vince and Joe Cunetto, wearing smocks of the period, surrounded by potions and liniments. The founding brothers, registered pharmacists until the day they died, started cooking and serving lunches with only four bowls and three spoons between them. "You can't leave a pharmacy," says Vince's wife, Nancy, who worked with them at the Southwest and Macklind drugstore for ten years. "After they made a big pot of minestrone or lentil soup (items still on today's menu), they invited local doctors or traveling salesmen to sit down and join them." Discovering a gold mine in the popularity of their dishes, the brothers rented the house across the street and opened Cunetto House of Pasta in 1974. "From day one, their mission was, 'The right food at the right price,'" asserts Nancy. The two brothers, along with their two sisters, were born in St. Louis, but their parents had emigrated from Casteltermini, Sicily. The current owner, Frank Cunetto (Vince's son) remembers washing floors, busing, and waiting tables at age 14, when the restaurant opened. "My dad and uncle hardly turned a profit until 1975, when an article appeared in the *St. Louis Post-Dispatch* by food critic Joe Pollack, praising our food, prices, and service. Cunetto House of Pasta was launched," says the optimistic, articulate, and business-minded graduate from the University of Missouri.

"One thing that the brothers did right, initially, was to hire our executive chef, Charlie Sanfilippo." Charlie, whose mother was a Cunetto, was lured away from Stan & Biggies. The affable chef sits down and tells a colorful history of early local Italian restaurants. He describes what it was like growing up on the Hill, "where, if you did not say hello just right up the street, by the time you got down the street, your mother knew all about it."

Visiting Cunetto's (now double its original size), one can always listen to Frank, Nancy, and Charlie reminisce. The place has a comfortable, close-knit family feel with friends and neighbors working and visiting together in harmony. All the best that this Italian neighborhood has to offer is found here. It started with Vince and Joe moving over and making room for one more at their backroom table. This spirit of hospitality still exists and affirms why, in the future, the lines will continue to curl around Cunetto's, the House of Pasta Joe and Vince built.

RECIPES | Cunetto's

LINGUINI TUTTO MARE

When asked about his signature dish, linguini tutto mare, which he created, Charlie elaborates. "Once on a slow, cold night, I was bored and put together this seafood pasta which has been copied coast to coast. I called Vince to the back and said 'Try it.' He tasted it and said, 'This is going on the menu.'" What is the secret to his tutto mare? "Clams that are rinsed well — I use quality shrimp and quality clam meat. I start the pasta sauce with a chicken broth — and add the butter in at the last minute. The ingredients used in Italian cooking are simple yet powerful," he reveals.

INGREDIENTS

8 oz. chicken broth
5 oz. chopped clams
6 oz. crabmeat
4 oz. mushrooms
6 oz. butter
1 tsp. crushed garlic
2 tbsp. chopped parsley
1 lb. linguini
salt and pepper to taste

Cook linguini according to "Cooking Pasta" below.

While pasta is cooking, place all the sauce ingredients in a pot and simmer for approximately five minutes. When pasta is al dente, strain and add to prepared sauce. Simmer for an additional three minutes and serve.

SERVES 4

COOKING PASTA

Here are some basic principles to ensure success. Step one — the pan and the water: use a light thin pan, such as aluminum, so the water can come quickly to a boil. The bottom of the pan should be flat, without dents, so the water gets the maximum amount of heat. The pan should have a capacity of six quarts. Every pound of pasta needs at least four quarts of water to swim in. This also allows the pieces to remain separated and it washes away excess starch to prevent the pasta from becoming gummy or gluey. Even when cooking one quarter pound, use a large pan and three quarts of water. If you cook two pounds of pasta, you are asking for trouble. When the water is boiling rapidly, add salt generously. Salt seals in the pasta flavor. Two tablespoons of table salt is recommended for four quarts of water and a pound of pasta. The water should taste salty. As to adding oil to the water, the answer is no. Add only a tablespoon of oil to boiling lasagna noodles. The oiled surface makes these noodles easier to handle. Otherwise, oil can interfere with the absorption of the sauce.

Cunetto's | RECIPES

CAVATELLI CON POMODORO

"This happened on one of those days when we were back in the kitchen experimenting, trying to come up with recipes. This became one of my favorites because it's a cream pasta that is still light. What I've found through the years is when customers come for lunch, they're concerned about their waistlines, but at night everybody just wants to eat," he says smiling. "The last three or four years, our big item at night is capellini with tomato sauce—just a light tomato sauce. Nothing to it. Lots of people have been eating it."

INGREDIENTS
1 lb. cavatelli (shell pasta)
3 cups mushrooms (sliced)
5 or 6 fresh medium-sized tomatoes
1/2 lb. butter
1/2 qt. half & half
2 tsp. minced garlic
2 tbsp. fresh parsley (chopped)
2 cups freshly grated parmesan cheese

Bring water to a boil and cook cavatelli according to "Cooking Pasta" instructions on page 168. While pasta is cooking, cut tomatoes in quarters. Strain the pasta and add the tomatoes, mushrooms, butter, and half & half, garlic and parsley to the drained pasta.

Cook on high heat stirring slowly until it boils. Lower heat to medium and let simmer until mixture thickens. Remove from the stove and slowly add the parmesan cheese until sauce clings to the pasta. Add salt and pepper to taste.

SERVES 4

Italian Food Facts

The best way to eat a good tomato is to cut it in slices or chunky wedges and dress it with extra-virgin olive oil, salt and pepper. Oregano or basil leaves and a touch of garlic add to the pleasure.

Sun-dried tomatoes are the legacy of frugal Italian peasants, who put to good use the abundant summer tomato harvest by drying the fresh tomatoes in the sun; that is the reason for their intense fragrance. Sun-dried tomatoes imported from Italy are preserved in extra-virgin olive oil.

Cunetto's | RECIPES

Linguini alla Pavarotti

In the 1980s, Vince Cunetto was listening to Pavarotti (a guest on the Johnny Carson show) describe his favorite meal. Vince got up from the TV and developed an adaptation that remains popular to this day on the House of Pasta menu.

Ingredients

- 1 lb. linguini
- 10-12 anchovies
- 1 tsp. red pepper
- 1/2 tsp. black pepper
- 3 tbsp. chopped parsley
- 2 tsp. chopped garlic
- 4 tbsp. olive oil
- 36-44 oz. of your favorite homemade marinara sauce or 44 oz. jar tomato sauce
- 1/3 stick butter
- parmesan cheese

Cook linguini according to "Cooking Pasta" instructions on page 168. Heat olive oil over medium heat, sauté anchovies until they melt. Add garlic and parsley; cook for about two minutes. Add tomato sauce, red pepper and black pepper; simmer for 10 to 12 minutes. During the last two minutes of cooking time add the butter. Place pasta in a bowl, add sauce, and serve with parmesan cheese.

Serves 4

Italian Food Facts

Fresh anchovies are one of the most delicate fish of the Mediterranean. They are caught only at the time of the waning moon. Their delicate flavor is perfect for a light luncheon. The best way to experience the anchovy is raw, simply fileted, splitting open their attractive blue-green back and silver sides, and marinating them for several hours in lemon juice. They are a treat cooked briefly in olive oil, with garlic and herbs.

Pasta is a generic term for all the multitude of products made from semolina and water. Semolina is the golden, sugar-fine flour made from the heart of durum wheat. This is the hardest and purest of all the wheats.

LENTIL SOUP

This recipe is believed to be a combination of both Charlie's (Rosalee Cunetto) and Vince's (Carmella Insalacao-Cunetto) mothers' specialties. At the restaurant this lentil soup is served every Thursday for lunch — ten gallons are prepared and enjoyed. Volume is a key to Cunetto's success. According to the ebullient Chef Charlie, in one day Cunetto's goes through four wheels of parmesan cheese (80 pounds) and 280 pounds of pasta (ten pounds per pot). Three days claim 65 gallons of both tomato and meat sauces. "I never skimp on any product, declared the chef. Quality stays high. I fight price increases all the time. That's my job." There are over one hundred people employed at Cunetto's.

Ingredients
- 2 oz. olive oil
- 1 cup chopped green onion
- 1/2 lb. dried split peas
- 1/2 lb. lentils
- 2 cups finely chopped broccoli
- 2 pkg. frozen spinach

Start with two pots that combined will equal about 5 gallons. Put one ounce of olive oil in each pot.

Pot #1: Sauté one cup chopped green onion in olive oil. Add two quarts of water and add 1/2 pound dried split peas and 1/2 pound lentils.

Pot #2: Add two quarts water, two cups of chopped broccoli and two packages of frozen spinach (or fresh chopped).

Cook both pots, salt and pepper to taste. Pot #2 will cook down faster than Pot #1 so turn off after 1/2 hour or so. Cook peas and lentils until they melt down completely. Add more water from time to time as needed. When both have cooked down, combine both pots and cook 10 minutes more to blend well. Don't be afraid to add more water if it gets too thick. (You can also sauté some garlic with onions and add to the final product.)

Serves 8

From the earliest recipes, Italian soups have included a whole variety of herbs, which was a reflection of the Italians' interest in and knowledge of the nutritive and curative properties of herbs. Even today in spring, you will still see hundreds of people in the fields gathering wild herbs and greens for the cooking pot.

Keep in mind the Italian expression, "What you put in there, you will find" (Quello che si mette, si trova) meaning that the ingredients you add to a dish will be tasted, so they must be good. In this case, they should taste Italian.

RECIPES — Cunetto's

BISTECCA ALLA SICILIANA

The origin of this dish is beef modiga, the Sicilian favorite. Charlie explains, "When emigrants came to the U.S., they were overwhelmed with the amount of meat available, a rare commodity in their birthplace. Cunetto's Bistecca alla Siciliana demonstrates how to take an everyday strip steak and, using their own homemade sauce, 'gourmet it up!'"

MARINADE
- 1 cup olive oil
- 1 tsp. garlic
- 2 lemons, juiced
- 1 tbsp. chopped parsley
- 1 tsp. salt
- 1 tsp. pepper

SICILIANA SAUCE
- 4 oz. chicken stock
- 1 oz. white wine
- 1 oz. lemon juice
- 1/2 stick butter
- flour for roux
- 1 cup sliced mushrooms
- 1 tsp. chopped garlic
- 1/2 tsp. black pepper

Marinate strip steak (or steak of your choice) for 20 minutes. Roll steak in one cup seasoned bread crumbs. Cook steak to desired doneness, being careful not to burn the bread crumbs.

In a saucepan combine chicken stock, white wine, and lemon juice. Bring to a simmer. Add garlic and pepper. Bring to a boil. Divide 1/2 stick butter into quarters. Roll butter in flour and press flour into butter. Add dredged butter to sauce one quarter at a time and briskly whisk this roux until completely incorporated into the sauce. After sauce thickens pour over steak.

SERVES 4

Italian Food Facts

To test the frying oil for the perfect frying temperature add a small piece of bread or a few bread crumbs to the oil. If the oil sizzles and the bread turns golden almost immediately, you can begin to fry.

During the 16th and 17th centuries, Italian cooking reached an incredible degree of complication and elaborateness. That was the era in which butter, ice, and sugar sculpture reached their height. Meat was served in such a way that the animal still appeared to be alive, and the feathers of birds were put back on after the birds were cooked.

Cunetto's | RECIPES

RECIPES | *Cunetto's*

SPAGHETTINI CON BROCCOLI

This is a variation on one of Rosalee Cunetto's prized dishes.

INGREDIENTS
1 lb. spaghettini
8 oz. package of frozen broccoli
1/2 stick butter
1 cup parmesan cheese
1 tsp. crushed garlic
5 oz. fresh mushrooms
3/4 quart half & half cream
salt and pepper

Bring water to a boil and add the spaghettini and cook according to "Cooking Pasta" instructions on page 168. While pasta is cooking, place half & half, butter, garlic, and mushrooms in a saucepan and simmer for ten minutes. Add the broccoli and bring to a boil. Add salt and pepper to taste. Stir in the pasta to this sauce and bring to a boil or until sauce thickens.

Remove from the stove and gradually add the cheese to obtain a creamy consistency and serve.

SERVES 4

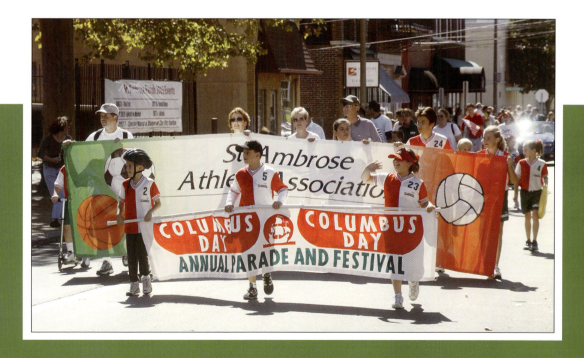

Cunetto's | RECIPES

Chicken Spedini

Thursday nights were reserved for beef spedini, and Vince, noting the success, decided to try the same recipe with chicken. It became so popular that chicken spedini now has its own home—Wednesday night dinner. "We go through 125 servings every Wednesday!" declares Charlie.

Ingredients

*6-8 oz. boneless chicken breasts
  cut into 1-inch pieces*
1 cup olive oil
1 cup white wine
1/2 cup parmesan cheese
1/2 cup bread crumbs
1/2 tsp. salt
1/2 tsp. black pepper
1/3 tsp. red pepper
2 tbsp. parsley

Sauce

1 lb. melted butter
1 cup lemon juice

Place all ingredients (except butter and lemon juice) in a large bowl and marinate for one hour. Place the chicken on a skewer and broil for eight to ten minutes.

Prepare sauce by infusing together butter and lemon juice. Ladle over the cooked chicken and serve.

Serves 6

RECIPES | Cunetto's

CHICKEN MARSALA

INGREDIENTS

8 oz. boneless breast of chicken
3 tbsp. Italian-seasoned bread crumbs
3 tbsp. olive oil
4 oz. beef stock
1 oz. Marsala wine
2 oz. tomato sauce
1/4 cup sliced mushrooms
1 tbsp. butter
1/8 cup flour

Bread boneless breast of chicken with bread crumbs. Saute in 2-3 tablespoons of olive oil over medium heat. In saucepan bring beef stock, Marsala wine and tomato sauce to a boil. Roll butter in flour and press flour into butter. Add dredged butter to sauce and briskly whisk until this roux is completely incorporated into the sauce. After the sauce thickens, dip sautéed chicken into sauce on both sides. Plate it. Ladle remaining sauce on top of chicken. Veal or beef may be substituted.

SERVES 1

A great story, but not necessarily true, is that of Alfredo, the owner of the celebrity-filled restaurant in Rome, Italy, which became internationally famous for its fettuccini Alfredo. The colorful, mustached restauranteur was invited to the St. Louis World's fair in 1904 to reproduce his renowned dish. He had his chefs bundle up many pounds of flour and dozens of eggs for making the tender pasta. He brought his own butter and cheese. When the chefs prepared the recipe in St. Louis and presented him with a dish for tasting he exclaimed, "I should have brought the water!"

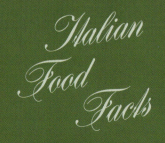
Italian Food Facts

The fruit of the ancient olive tree has played a significant role in the lives of the Mediterranean people. Kings and priests have been anointed with olive oil; Roman athletes oiled themselves to make their muscles supple; noble ladies used it to keep their skin soft.

Cunetto's | RECIPES

DITALINI CON PISELLI

Charlie inherited this recipe from his mother, and from her mother before her. It has its roots in the common-sense practice of cooking with what one has.

INGREDIENTS

1 lb. ditalini
2 bunches chopped green onions
2 cups frozen peas
3 tbsp. olive oil
parmesan cheese
salt and pepper to taste

Cook pasta according to "Cooking Pasta" instructions on page 168. In a one-quart saucepan, heat olive oil and sauté the green onions until soft, add peas and stir for about one minute. Cover peas with water and bring to a boil. Cook until soft. Salt and pepper to taste. Place pasta in a bowl, add peas and toss. Top with parmesan cheese and serve.

Tip: If you like your pasta moist, add a little of the pasta water.

SERVES 4

CHICKEN CARDINALE

"We put a little tomato sauce on top to represent the Catholic Cardinal's hat. This recipe came from Andrino's, and later showed up at Rich and Charlie's Trattoria." Charlie also remembers his first job as a busboy at Tony's, "where everybody started their restaurant career. After Tony's, I parked cars for Andrino's where Dominic's is today. Andrino's innovative pasta ideas greatly influenced Italian cooking in St. Louis. He introduced cream pastas, fettuccine, and many Italian dishes to the area. I used to watch him cook and do his magic. I learned a lot. Rich and Charlie (Richard Ronzio and Charlie Mugavero) also worked at Andrino's as waiters."

INGREDIENTS

4 oz. chicken stock
1 oz. white wine
1 oz. lemon juice
1 tbsp. butter
1/8 cup flour
1/4 cup sliced mushrooms
1/8 cup frozen peas
2 oz. grated provel cheese
1 8 oz. breaded, fried, boneless chicken breast

Fry boneless breast of chicken as per Chicken Marsala recipe on page 178. Bring chicken stock, white wine and lemon juice to a boil. Roll butter in the flour. Add peas and butter to sauce. Whip briskly to incorporate the butter before adding cheese. Dip the chicken breast into the thickened sauce on both sides. Plate it. Pour remaining sauce over the dish.

SERVES 1

Cunetto's | RECIPES

MINESTRONE SOUP

This soup was one of the original delights served by the Cunetto brothers in their pharmacy days. The recipe is commonly acknowledged as Vince's, who originally got it from his mother.

INGREDIENTS

4 cloves garlic crushed
2 oz. virgin olive oil
1 medium onion chopped
1/2 cup chopped parsley
2 carrots chopped
1 head escarole chopped
1/2 head endive chopped
1/2 head cabbage chopped
8 oz. broccoli chopped
8 oz. cauliflower chopped
1 can plum tomatoes chopped
2 medium-sized zucchini chopped
2 qts. beef broth
salt and pepper to taste

OPTIONAL

8 oz. baby lima beans
1 can chickpeas
2 diced potatoes

In a stockpot, sauté garlic and onions in olive oil. Add two quarts of beef broth and bring to a boil. Add all of the vegetables (chopped) and bring to a boil with lid on the pot. Cook until all vegetables are tender. Season with salt and pepper.

SERVES 4-6

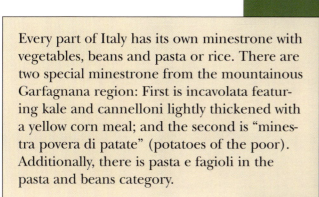

Every part of Italy has its own minestrone with vegetables, beans and pasta or rice. There are two special minestrone from the mountainous Garfagnana region: First is incavolata featuring kale and cannelloni lightly thickened with a yellow corn meal; and the second is "minestra povera di patate" (potatoes of the poor). Additionally, there is pasta e fagioli in the pasta and beans category.

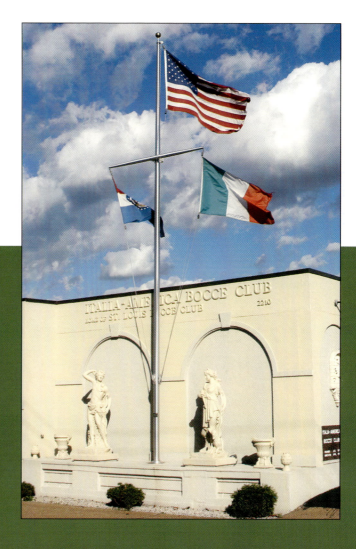

HISTORY | *The Now Years*

Aerial view of the Hill region.

CHAPTER THREE: THE NOW YEARS

After the war years and the subsequent recovery and reconstruction during the 1950s, the citizens of the Hill had attained a renewal of their identity. Pride in their Italian culture and heritage could readily be seen throughout their neighborhood and in the spirit of all their festivities. Similarly, there was a renewal in Italian food, as Hill restaurants and markets began attracting people from near and far in search of a truly unique Italian experience.

The crowds at Hill Day in front of St. Ambrose Church. No one expected the tremendous response for this event.

HISTORY | *The Now Years*

HILL DAY

The first Hill Day celebration was held on August 15, 1965. Although its original purpose was to celebrate the Centennial of the City of Saint Louis, it was a great opportunity to demonstrate the culture and warm hospitality of the Hill community.

Festivities began at 12 noon, lasting until 10:00 p.m. Multiple booths featured souvenirs, knit and quilt works, embroidery and cut-out work, and hand-crafted ornaments. Food preparations were demonstrated and sold to eager visitors. Savory dishes of Italian-style eggplants, ravioli, salciccia, mostaccioli, and meatballs were available. Other booths offered delicious Italian cookies and homemade jams and jellies. Additional Hill Day features included Italian folk dancing and singing. Beautifully decorated floats were driven through the streets of the Hill and the evening ended with spectacular fireworks.

The Hill Day's Festivities were discontinued in 1979. Throughout its existence, more than 150,000 visitors were given the opportunity to enjoy the culture and traditions of the Hill's Italian heritage.

Above: Crowds gather to celebrate Hill Day's Festivities in 1976.

Crowds are entertained by Hill Day performers in 1965.

HILL 2000

The Hill Improvement Association was formed in 1969, with its primary goal to improve several areas throughout the Hill. Homes needed repairs, streets and alleys were to be kept clean, and the residents' safety was always a major concern.

At that time, Reverend Salvatore Polizzi recognized the need for a stronger, more unified association. Together with William Nardoni, the assistant vice president of Southwest Bank, they contacted Hill businessmen to form a Board. Each business was to contribute $1,000 of assistance, and their contributions served as incentives for the Hill's residents to do likewise.

Members of the first Board were: Dr. Charles Montani (President), Reverend Salvatore Polizzi (Vice President), and John Berra (Treasurer) who was the owner of Berra's Paint Store. The name Hill 2000 was chosen to point to the future with the hope that the Hill would continue to grow and remain a vital part of the City of Saint Louis.

Hill 2000 was essentially a combined community effort to preserve the stability and wholesomeness of the neighborhood. With Reverend Polizzi's unbounded enthusiasm, the Hill 2000's Board members propelled the community into action. The goal was simply to keep alive the culture and traditions of the Hill's founders, the Italian immigrants.

A constitution and a set of bylaws was drawn up. The group's purpose, stated in the bylaws (Article III, Section I), was "to initiate programs and to plan effectively and creatively for the future welfare of the area, in regard to the continued quality of community life." The phrase "Pride Builds" was then adopted as the theme for this organization.

The young people of the Hill constructed various floats for the Hill Day Parade. The "Roman Ruins" was a popular float concept, receiving cheers from the crowd.

HISTORY | The Now Years

The Hill Day Musical Trio was just one of the numerous musical acts which entertained the crowds over the years. Identified (L-R) are Al Gaia, Charles "Skip" Torretta, and Salvatore Finocchiaro.

Gino Mariani, a philosopher, poet, and photographer, enjoys the Hill Day's activities.

Skip Torretta, a composer and director, is accompanied by Ms. Elaine Fassi.

Mr. Robert "Bootsie" DeMattei (far right) announces the next performance; a choral group comprised of young schoolgirls.

BREAK A LEG

In the mid-1950s, Reverend Salvatore Polizzi was instrumental in creating the Saint Ambrose Theatrical Club, with its members called the Ambrosians. Their first musical was *The Boyfriend* in 1956. It united the successful collaboration between Skip Torretta, the musical director, and Ms. Patricia Merlo, the drama director and choreographer. They soon launched the entire neighborhood into an exciting venture, exploring the realm of creativity and artistry. Becoming a community project, neighborhood artists, carpenters, and electricians joined together to help make each production a success.

Together Merlo and Torretta produced many plays, including Torretta's original musicals: *Duck, the Garlic's Flying* (1967), *Apple Fever* (1972), *Remember When* (1978), *O Mona, Mon Ami* (1997), and *Break a Leg* (1997). Their group also performed U.S.O. shows in St. Louis at Union Station, in conjunction with Veterans Day in the 1980s.

Perhaps the most important aspect of these productions was the fact that the entire community came together–the young and the old, talented veterans, and stage amateurs. The only prerequisite was simply to volunteer and to be interested. There was always a spot for everyone, and it was a great opportunity to meet your neighbors and, especially, to have fun.

Merlo and Torretta's group puts on a U.S.O. performance.

The action stops for a cast photo. Pictured (L-R) are Dennis Cassani, Jim Merlo, Reverend Sal Polizzi, Maryann Marnati-Polizzi, Claire Parino (standing), Pat Merlo (sitting), and Dorothy Palazzola-Gambaro.

A rehearsal scene from Skip Torretta's original musical play, Duck, The Garlic's Flying.

History | *The Now Years*

HURDLES

The Hill community has had to overcome external threats which have endangered its very existence. In 1956, the Federal Highway Department planned for Interstate 44 to run directly through the northern section of the Hill. The Highway Department bought properties on Pattison Avenue and began to demolish homes. They also planned for an additional ramp, which would have razed even more residences as well as cutting off 150 houses from the rest of the community. The Hill residents wanted an overpass which joined these two areas, as well as an emergency entrance. Action was taken and a committee was formed. Its leaders were: the former associate pastor of Saint Ambrose Church, Reverend Sal Polizzi; City Alderman Alfred Giuffrida; Eugene Mazzuca; Missouri State Representative Paul Berra; and City Treasurer Paul Turin. The committee flew to Washington D.C. to meet with the Secretary of Transportation, John Volpi.

Reverend Polizzi offered to give $50,000 of Hill 2000 money to offset the cost of the overpass. At the hearing, Volpi said he was familiar with the Hill neighborhood and was impressed by the condition of its homes. He was also impressed with the fact that a small community would offer to give money to the federal government to help defray any extra expenses. Their trip to Washington brought national media attention to the Hill. Finally, due to the

The Immigrant Statue, sculpted by Rudy Torrini in 1971.

excellent leadership and the stark determination of the Hill's occupants, a victorious outcome took place.

A second obstacle to overcome was a drive-in movie theater, planned to be built on Wilson Avenue. Allowing this to happen would have caused a threat to the relative quiet of the Hill's residential area. Once again, Reverend Sal Polizzi recognized the need to organize the community to oppose the plan. In a meeting with the real estate company, citizens strongly voiced their concern. The voice of the people was heard and the drive-in project was defeated.

Another threat which occurred in the 1960s was of a different nature. Alderman Alfred Giuffrida discovered at City Hall that the National Lead Company was trying to obtain a permit from the Board of Public Service to pump slurry (a watery mixture of industrial waste) into the old clay mines which are honey-combed throughout the Hill region. Planning to pour 40,000 gallons per day into these mines, it would ultimately threaten the basic physical structure of the Hill.

Alderman Giuffrida immediately went to the president of the Board of Public Service and demanded a public hearing before a permit could be issued. He then contacted a fellow Committee member, Paul Berra, and informed him of the situation. After discussing the problem, they spoke to Reverend Polizzi and State Senator Larry Lee at Saint Ambrose Church. The senator, also an attorney, offered to help. Several bus loads of Hill residents went to the hearing at City Hall and their objections were presented by their leaders. The National Lead Company was denied its permit and, once again, these indomitable sons and daughters of immigrants were successful in their efforts to protect their cherished home.

HISTORY | The Now Years

FEAST OF SAINT JOSEPH

One of the Hill's most beloved saints is Saint Joseph, a humble carpenter from Nazareth. On March 19, many show their devotion to this saint by preparing lavish dinners and sharing with the needy. The Sicilians believe it is a date when its people were sent rain during a severe drought which had caused many to die of starvation. This feast is a special day, created to honor Saint Joseph for answered prayers.

Even today in Sicily, every village selects an orphan boy, a young girl, and an old carpenter to portray the Holy Family weeks in advance. Then, on March 19, they mount mules while wearing simple garments to parade through the village, where they are cheered and given gifts of money and food.

At St. Ambrose Church, the feast was initiated in 1968 by Reverend Polizzi, and it continues to this day. A beautiful Saint Joseph's Altar is adorned with magnificent embroidered cut-out work, handmade by the Hill's elderly women. Surrounding the altar are displays of pastries, braided breads, and traditional Saint Joseph dishes.

Saint Joseph tables are often set up by people in their own homes. The priests then go to these homes and bless the table. A symbolic dish of uncooked fava beans is also set on the table to represent the legendary famine's only available food item. Any donation received from guests is forwarded to assist people in need. The Saint Joseph's Altar is a timeless tradition left to the people of the Hill by their Italian ancestors, and it has been continued to ensure its preservation.

(L-R) Over the years, Anna Berra, Gina Chiodini, Rita Ranzini, and many other talented women from the Hill have traditionally embroidered exquisite cut-out work for the altar of St. Ambrose Church.

The Now Years | HISTORY

Mrs. Mary Parisi (on right) watches over her daughter as she shapes honey balls to form pignolata – special Italian sweets!

(L-R) Agnes Gorla, Rachel Migneco, and Mary Torretta stand ready to distribute St. Joseph's blessed bread.

Grace Caruso vigorously kneads dough for Hill Day cookies.

The magnificent St. Joseph's Altar is decorated with beautiful flowers, breads formed in various shapes, and many delicious Italian cookies.

191

HISTORY | The Now Years

SERVICE

Whenever Hill residents meet with misfortune or privation, the church and her community strives to lighten their burdens with generous contributions and continuous support. As early as 1914, the Saint Vincent DePaul Society of Saint Ambrose Church assisted families with special needs.

Today, its benevolent works continue by assisting with utility payments, food vouchers, clothing, and procuring medical help. The members of this society raise funds each month from the parishioners of Saint Ambrose Church. Members of the parish also take part in canned food and clothing drives, which are sponsored by the Saint Vincent DePaul Society.

The Sick and Elderly Program was initiated in 1970 by Rosemarie and John Bianchi. The toughest hurdle which this couple faced was convincing the proud elderly residents of the Hill to allow them to help. Today, the program continues to be operated by the Bianchi family. The Sick and Elderly Program offers more than material support. In keeping with the rich history, heritage, and true spirit of the Italian immigrant, this organization offers love, loyalty, and respect for Hill residents.

Those brought up in the Hill have served their community in many ways. Neighbors helping neighbors is a common practice. When a need was discovered, family members could be confident that help was not far away.

Above: (L-R) Jim Torrisi, Angelo Bianchi, and Bob Galli prepare meatballs and pasta for Hill Day.
Below: The St. Ambrose Senior Citizen Quilters and Crafters prepare their work for the annual LaFesta Celebration.

The Now Years | HISTORY

BERRA PARK

Berra Park is named for Louis "Midge" Berra. Berra served the Hill community as an alderman and ward boss for the 24th Ward. Berra was also the community's spokesperson and main benefactor.

This five-acre park was originally called Vigo Park, when the land was purchased from the City of St. Louis in 1945. It was renamed Berra Park in 1965, and it continues to serve as a site for baseball and soccer games, fund-raising picnics, and an annual summer day camp sponsored by the Shaw Community School Center. Since 1985, Community Education Director Joseph Torrisi has conducted an All-Day Camp during the summer in Berra Park. The program began simply, with fifteen children participating. Today, its enrollment has increased to 250. The curriculum includes arts, crafts, games, and field trips.

One exceptional activity introduced by Mr. Torrisi and his staff is the Challenger Baseball Game, played by children who are physically disabled. In the past, the match was opened by Christopher Bianchi, a special needs student, singing our country's *National Anthem*. At the game's conclusion, Mayor Francis Slay awarded each participant with a medal, so that everyone is a winner! In keeping with the Hill's spirit of caring and giving, activities such as these, along with several other similar ones, are welcomed by the community.

His Honor the Mayor of St. Louis, Francis G. Slay, places an award on a young ballplayer after the Challenger Baseball Game.

Joe Torrisi bows his head as Christopher Bianchi leads the crowd in singing the National Anthem.

Long before Berra Park, in the early 1930s, club members from the Stags and Hawks organizations competed in a Turkey Bowl Soccer Game on Thanksgiving Day. Today, over a half-century later, the tradition continues. Young adults are matched up against the Hill's older veterans. Grade school children also have teams which participate in this yearly event.

HISTORY | *The Now Years*

(L-R) Adriana Fazio and her daughter, Dianna, get a hug from the great T.V. cook, Mario Batali.

The Giro della Montagna is an annual bicycle race which usually takes place over the Labor Day weekend. Participants travel from all over the United States for the opportunity to compete along the Hill's streets.

(L-R) Monsignor Polizzi and Reverend Bommarito celebrate the renaming of the 5400 block of Elizabeth to Hall of Fame Place, in honor of (L-R) Yogi Berra and Joe Garagiola. Joining the celebration are their wives, Carmen Berra and Audrey Garagiola.

The Now Years | HISTORY

THE MOVIE
THE GAME OF THEIR LIVES

In the spring of 2003, Hollywood invaded the Hill. With a little movie magic, director David Anspaugh and screenwriter Angelo Pizzo whisked the entire neighborhood back to the 1950s. During this exciting event, the Hill's local inhabitants felt like they were caught in some sort of a time warp!

Thousands of people descended upon Shaw School, responding to an open call for extras in the major motion picture, *The Game of Their Lives*. Based on the book by Geoffrey Douglas, it is an exciting, edge-of-your-seat story about a group of Americans who pulled off one of soccer's most stunning upsets; defeating the powerhouse English team in the 1950 World Cup games. The Americans, as the undisputed underdogs, were listed as a 500-to-1 shot by London bookmakers.

Many parts of this movie were filmed on the Hill by transforming its homes, businesses, and streets into a 1950s neighborhood. The roadways were crowded with tourists equipped with cameras so they could take pictures of the "movie on the Hill."

Local residents are especially proud since five players on the American team were boys from the Hill. Frank Borghi, Frank "Pee-Wee" Wallace, Charles "Lefty" Colombo, Gino Pariani, and Bobby Annis were able to prove the well-known maxim which is often repeated by immigrants, regardless of their ethnicity: "In America, you can be anything you want."

The producers put up a false front on the empty lot across from St. Ambrose Church. The popular Hill historian, Roland DeGregorio, is seen sitting in a chair, watching the action.

Above: A group of Hill extras take part in the "funeral scene."
Right: The cameras roll in front of St. Ambrose Church.

HISTORY | The Hill

CONTRIBUTORS

Bill Anselmo
Joanne Arpiani
Dorothy Bartoni
Edward Berra
John Berra
Lance Berra
Lawrence Berra
Reverend Vincent
 Bommarito
Frank & Rosemarie Borghi
Carm Cacciatore
Mary Calcaterra
Theresa Carnaghi
Isabelle Ceriotti
Chuck Chiodini
Carla Colombo
Assunta Della Croce
Laura Della Croce
Eugene Cucchi
Roland DeGregorio
Dora DiGregorio
Vincent & Virginia
 DiRaimondo
Constance Economon
Adriana Fazio
Charles Fazio
Carolyn Feder
Mary Felix
Charles & Rose Ferrario
Marilyn Ferrario
Gilda Ferronato
Ben & Gloria Gambaro
Clem Garavaglia
Louis Garavaglia
Frank Gianino
Pauline Gianino
Charlie & Annie Gitto
Charlie Gitto, Jr.
Al & Jean Giuffrida

Theresa Giudici
Gloria Grifferro
Edith Grassi
Johanna Grimoldi
Anna Jo Hof
Ermanno & Julie Imo
John Italiano
Rose Kelso
Donna Kemper
Anna Lahrman
Joseph Lonigro
Rich & Terri LoRusso
Judy Marcalini
Eugene Mariani
Joseph Mazzuca
Mary Mae Mazzuca

Albina McFall
James Merlo
Pat Merlo
Rita Meriotti
Rachelle Migneco
Camille Miriani
Sister Anthony Novara
Rosemary Parentin
Victor Passanisi
Armando Passetti
Julia Pastori
Hope Peluso
Josephine & Dr. Robert
 Pisoni
Monsignor Salvatore Polizzi
Sister Eleanor Pozzo

Linda Pozza
Mike Pozzo
Shirley Puricelli
Rose Restelli
Jennie Rhodus
Nicholas Riggio
Mary Ronzio
Robert Ruggeri
Sam Rumbolo
Anita Russo
Mary Ann Sack
Charlie Sanfilippo
Carol Steltzer
Larry Tornetto
Paul Torno
Joseph Torrisi

Diane Urzi
Carole Valli
Angeline Venegoni
Anna Rose Venegoni
Jim & Faye Venegoni
John Viviano
Mary Zagarri
Virginia Zienta-Barbeau
Sara Zona

The staff and students of St. Ambrose School in 1943.

196

ACKNOWLEDGEMENTS

First and foremost, I would like to thank the people of the Hill community who, as always, have embraced every new undertaking with enthusiasm. They have opened up their hearts and homes to the service of this project. Without them, this book would not have been possible as their support and encouragement were key factors.

In particular, I'd like to give special thanks and appreciation to Monsignor Sal Polizzi, whose deep love and unbridled devotion to the Hill and its people has, once again, prompted my personal participation. Also, to Reverend Vincent Bommarito, the pastor of St. Ambrose Church, for his generous cooperation in giving us his time and talent; to Patricia Merlo and Jim Merlo whose stark determination led them to delve into the church and Hill archives to unearth the photographs of the early immigrants; and to my niece, Faye Venegoni, for her support and editing skills. On the production end, thanks to Brad Baraks and his staff at G. Bradley Publishing for their expertise in creating this handsome publication; and to Jim Kersting, of Voyles Studio, for his exceptional color photography. Last, but certainly not least, I'd like to give my deepest appreciation to my husband, Dominic Marfisi, for his unending patience and encouragement.

Eleanore Berra Marfisi

Note: The following publications were used in researching the history chapters: *Nova Chiesa Italiana Di Sant'Ambrogio, Historical Review*, St. Ambrose Church, 1907-1943; *The Hill: The Ethnic Heritage of an Urban Neighborhood* (Washington University); *The Hill* (Missouri Historical Society); *Hill 2000* newspapers, 1971-1981; *Crusader Clarion*, 1944-1950; and other incidental resources.

HISTORY | The Hill

STAFF

The production staff for *The Hill: Its History, Its Recipes* has enjoyed its many months of designing, editing, collecting photographs, and conducting interviews. Our sincerest thanks to the Hill community for your patience and understanding as you welcomed us into your kitchens, your homes, and your hearts. Pictured are (L-R) Gloria Baraks, Diane Kramer, Michael Bruner, Jim Kersting, Faye Venegoni, and Dominic Marfisi. On the steps are Darlene Weber, Brad Baraks, and the author, Eleanore Berra Marfisi. Photograph taken, and porch provided, by Tom Mullen.

THEN & NOW

Berra's Furniture Store	Bertarelli Cutlery
Serra's Drugstore	Law Offices
Family Theatre	DiGregorio's warehouse
Rose's Tavern	Lorenzo's Trattoria
Savoy Garden	Vitale's Bakery
Consolino's Market	Zia's Restaurant
Merlo's (Forchet's) Tavern	Milo's Tavern
Rumbolo's Market	Adriana's
Gioia's Market	Gioia's Deli
Fair Mercantile	Modesto Bar & Restaurant, antique store
Rau Store	Viviano & Sons Retail Grocers, Inc.
Riggio Bank	Shaw's Coffee Ltd.
Big Club Hall	photography studio
Colombo's Tavern	Gian-Tony's On the Hill
Panther's Club	Marconi Bakery
Columbia Theatre	private residence & art studio
Monte's Tavern & Garden	DiGregorio's Italian Foods
Gitto's Shoe Store	Silver Bear Jewelry
Garavaglia's Market	Italian Imports
tin shop	Amighetti's (Hill location)

Epilogue

The Hill continues to stand as it always stood. Row upon row of shotgun houses still act as sentinels guarding and protecting their people. Majestic bells still solemnly summon her faithful to Saint Ambrose Church as they did a century ago.

Yet while the Hill has remained the same in many respects, it hasn't been able to halt the inevitable changes of time. The relative size of a three-room "shotgun" home, which used to house a large family of immigrants, did not entice their grandchildren to remain on the Hill. Many wished to move where larger homes were more available. Since the 1940s, the Veterans Administration and the Federal Housing Authority has made it possible for World War II veterans to purchase new and larger homes. Many took advantage of this opportunity and moved away from the Hill.

However, in recent years, many have returned to build a second floor on some of the old structures, or to simply build larger homes. Today, the narrow "shotgun" homes from the past share space with these larger homes, with several complexes of modern condominiums, and even a small subdivision of two-story three-bedroom homes. Young families have decided to finally come back to their roots.

As the residential and business areas have changed, so too has the cultural and occupational make-up of the Hill community. The post-war period brought about many of these changes, since the Hill was no longer an isolated community. Cultural boundaries began to break down when young men, after going off to war, experienced a world outside of their self-contained neighborhood. They no longer felt sheltered, so they went away to school and intermarriages with non-Italian families became more frequent. After receiving a better education than the previous generation, they became more financially secure. It was, indeed, a sign that this new generation were truly Americans.

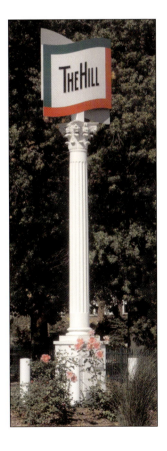

Thomas Wolfe, a twentieth-century American novelist, once said, "You can't go home again!" No doubt Thomas Wolfe never had the pleasure of experiencing life on the Hill. Anyone who has ever lived on the Hill can tell you that, returning to the old neighborhood is like truly going home again.

In looking back, we can see that the times have certainly changed. The children of our grandparents' children have changed. But their deep-rooted, intrinsic values have not changed. Many people can spend their entire lives not knowing who they are. The difference is people from the Hill know who they are as they have a strong sense of identity. They love and respect their roots. **They know they can always come back home again.**

Remembering the Hill

Keep a record of any stories or memories from your time spent on the Hill!